ARE YOU GOING TO EAT THAT?

Michael B Campbell

m c

WWW.MCWRITING.COM

FIRST EDITION

Library of Congress Cataloging-in-Publication Data

Campbell, Michael B.
    Are you going to eat that / Michael B Campbell.
ISBN 978-0-578-02750-0
  1. Humor — Alligators — Luggage — Tequila — Barbie

DESIGNED BY SARAH BELLAM

Printed in the United States of America

For my father and mother, Jack and June

CONTENTS

INTRODUCTION

I'VE LIVED only in Nebraska. That embarrasses me. Not that living in Nebraska is something to be ashamed of. Far from it. Nebraska is a state of plain beauty and adventure, all demurely hidden from the flat scar of Interstate 80, which bisects it. That highway provides the only perspective most visitors ever get of Nebraska as they try to make the trip from Denver to Chicago as fast as possible.

One can't understand the world without spending time crawling around in it. I'm the first to admit I don't understand the world, but I'm working on it, starting by crawling around in my own head.

For fifteen years I worked as a writer and editor at a newsletter publishing company. It was a small business, so I also gained valuable experience at customer service and how to properly push a mop.

We had customers all over the country. I began to notice geographic personality patterns from place to place. Southerners, for example, consider it rude to start talking business without a few pleasantries first. "Nebraska, huh? Why, it's mighty cold up there this time of year, eh?" a sales call would start, and end with "Well, y'all keep warm up there." Those on the West Coast ask a lot of questions but don't really care about your answers. "It comes out every month? Okay. By e-mail? Uh-huh. Does it come in a hardcopy version? Uh-huh — no, I only want the e-mail one." They just feel better for having done the research. East Coast callers start slowly at first, because they're not sure if anyone in the Midwest is literate. New Yorkers are the exception, talking so fast you're lucky to get the "hell" out of "hello" before they interrupt and get to the point. They want off the phone, and it's all one can do to get their order information before they hang up. They don't have time to find out whether I'm stupid or not.

Midwesterners genuinely want to learn something about you first, and openly share of ourselves in return. We are accustomed to doing business among friends. If you're a stranger, we prefer to make you a friend first:

"Thank you for calling. How can I help you?"

"This is Ben from XYZ in Fargo. How are you doing today?"

"Just fine, thank you. Too nice outside to be working. And you?"

"Fair to middlin'. My wife thought she broke her leg yesterday, but turns out it was just a bone bruise."

"Oooo, those heal slow. I bruised my heel last summer, and it took six months before it felt right again."

"Well, she deserves to be off her feet anway. She's always running. So, I read here that you have these newsletters..."

And every call ends with a return to the original chat: "...thank you for your order. And tell your wife to stay off that bruised leg. You take care now." (Nebraskans don't say *y'all*, unless they're pretending to be folksy. But they do pronounce *both* as *bolth*, and occasionally offer you an extra *r* in your *sugar* and *sherbet.)*

It was part of my job to e-mail art files to these disparate customers once a month. Internetiquette was not well defined then. It felt a little rude to send an art file without at least a little "how do you do," so I got in the habit of including a short personal message with each upload, something like that pre-business chat we would have had in real life. It wasn't much, just a paragraph or two, some observations from Nebraska, which can be an unusual viewpoint.

The writing sparked memories which, if they weren't funny then, were certainly funny now. God clearly has a sense of humor, and that comforts me, because the minute God stops finding humans entertaining, we're all in trouble.

Customers responded generously. Letters came back thanking me for putting a human touch on an otherwise impersonal subscription service. They shared their own reflections on the topic of the month. One charming couple from Arizona — Ol' Buzzards, they called themselves — continued to send me postcards from their RV travels around the country for years after they retired. They were no longer my customers, but we were still friends, after all.

When I sold the newsletter business and opened a music venue, the monthly observations became weekly ones, and the customer e-mail list grew. People cheerfully told me they didn't care who was performing at my club — they wanted to be on the list just to get the stories.

Every Tuesday I'd sit with my blank brain in front of my blank screen and think, what's so funny? Something always was. Occasionally I'd have a seed of an idea ahead of time, but usually not. Something always pushed its way out my fingers.

After a few years I had collected a sizeable bunch of essays. At the enthusiastic urging of friends I chose my favorites and wove them together into this collection. So now when people ask, "When are you going to write a book?" I can hit them up for money.

I have since sold the bar, but I kept the mailing list, and still send weekly essays. Nobody seems to mind (or even notice) that I'm not promoting shows anymore.

You can still read the weekly humor essays as they hatch, at the website below:

WWW.MCWRITING.COM

Be sure to leave a comment, say "Hi," get your two cents in. That's how we do things around here, anyway. 🐛

ARE YOU GOING
TO EAT THAT?

YOUR FINAL DESTINATION

MELANIE MCGUIRE WAS INDICTED FOR MURDERING her husband, after he washed ashore, in parts, on the Virginia coast. He was neatly packed into three trunks of his own matching monogrammed luggage.

I can only presume it was one of those matching sets with the various bag sizes: the big one probably for his torso, the smaller one (that kind which fits in the overhead bin) for appendages, and of course, the hand bag.

The story made Mrs. McGuire out to be something of a sadistic monster, but she couldn't have been too crazy. I thought there was some art to her methodology. She thought things out.

Arriving at your final destination in your own monogrammed bag seems tidy. Obviously, unless she marries another "W.T.M.," the luggage isn't of use to her any more. The bags are his. You can almost hear her voice as she tossed the bags overboard, or off the bridge, or however she did it: "Have a nice trip, Honey." Toss, splash. "Bon voyage." Toss, splash. "Don't forget your shoes — and your feet!"

And what is a casket, anyway, but a giant suitcase, minus only the little three-number padlock. Use your own luggage to reach your final destination and you can skip the concrete vault — just pack like you do for any long flight: wrap anything that leaks in plastic. And having twice been a pall-bearer, I can say the job would be much easier if, like suitcases, caskets had those little pull-out extension handles and nifty rollerblade wheels.

Judging from the ones I see at the airport, most people have bags that are plenty big enough. Heaven would be one giant baggage claim. Or should we still call it a terminal? ❦

ONE UGLY CAT

Since 1948 only seventeen people have been eaten by alligators. But last week alone three more made the list.

"By the time spring gets here," commented Arnold Brunell, wildlife biologist, "their activities increase quite a bit." I guess Dr. Brunell considers eating people an "activity."

When I was a kid, activities included shuffleboard and badminton. Even then, which was admittedly a long time ago, activities did not include eating each other.

One alligator victim reportedly had been jogging near a canal. My first thought was, "Wow, that was *not* her fault. She was already running." Indeed, nothing would make you pick up your pace more than having an alligator fall in behind you. But witnesses reported that they saw a woman who fit her description pausing along the shoreline, shoeless, dangling her sweet, fat little toes over the river. So there's that.

Afterwards authorities caught an alligator, and, hoping to prove its guilt, they opened it. But all they found inside were two tennis balls and a football. "Okay," I thought. *"Those* are activities."

Soon after, a second woman was killed while scuba diving. (Activity.) Authorities warned local residents against running, swimming, or practicing your serve near the water.

I was ready to declare that alligators are sports fans, but the next victim, a cocaine addict, was found with her arm bitten off. Witnesses heard her calling, "Here kitty, kitty, kitty..." I imagine this alligator bit her just on principle.

Authorities issued an updated warning against swimming, sports of all kinds, and feeding suspiciously ugly cats near a canal. They caught and opened three more alligators, which yielded a catcher's mitt, a pair of Reeboks, chrome dumbbells, a one pound can of Joe Weider's PowerMax Vanilla Protein Powder, a Nordic Trac, and a tin of Little Friskies.

So what do they do when they kill an animal and discover it wasn't the one that ate the missing victim? "Oh, sorry — guess it wasn't you. Go back to your normal activities." ❦

REBEL WITHOUT A CORK

"THAT HAD BETTER NOT BE TEQUILA." The Mexican customs agent ground her words through gritty teeth as she looked at Laura's hand, which was holding a bottle of tequila.

"No, it's not," I wanted to say on her behalf. "It's a special hammer to hit rude people on the head. Want to see how it works?" But Laura doesn't need any help with wisecracks, and I'm afraid of customs people in general, so I kept my mouth shut.

"Yes, it's tequila," Laura responded honestly, leaving off the implied *"...you idiot."*

"I hope you're not planning to take it on the airplane." Laura respects airline officials too, so more words were left unspoken. When she was ordered to dump the tequila out she complied, with a bit lip and a fat tear of frustration in her eye. She had anticipated a warm snifter of that expensive tequila, the thought carrying her through the long trip home after a busy week-long "destination wedding" in Cancún.

Our friend Raoul bought some nice tequila at the duty-free shop too, but it was still in his carry-on bag. We passed him in the zig-zag cattle line queued for the x-ray scanner, and when he asked what happened to her tequila, we shushed him. If they didn't search his bag, then maybe.... But they did search it, and told him he couldn't take it any further.

"That is *so* wrong," he complained. Raoul does not waste liquor. It would have killed him to pour it out. So he did what I would only dream of doing: he popped open the cap and upended the bottle into his mouth, chugging until bubbles coursed through it. Then he raised it up high in defiance, as if it were the head of Goliath, and yelled to the other weary travelers, "Who wants some tequila!?"

Raoul is a very big, very imposing man. Everyone froze, wanting a swig of that golden tequila but not wanting to draw the attention of the fierce little customs agent, who appeared ready to blow a hole in Raoul. To my shock, she repeated in her shrill Chihuahua bark, "Aneewan wan sam tah-KEE-la!?"

In unison the crowd exploded, *"TEQUILA!"* and cheered as the first guy in line behind Raoul accepted the bottle neck in his fist and knocked back a swig, then passed it back down the line. Twenty people later it made it to Laura and me, and we each took a pull. It felt hot and exciting in my throat. The bottle was two-thirds empty when I lost sight of it, still making comrades of us all.

Making a mental count of those who had wrapped their lips around it ahead me, I figure my mouth did the equivalent of kissing two big bald guys, a rugby player, a new husband and an attractive forty-ish Latina — about the same luck as I have here in Omaha. I prefer to observe rebellions from a safe distance, but in this case I'm glad I was close to the source, although there were some in the line I wouldn't kiss even if they were marinated in tequila.

We dubbed it The Great Tequila Rebellion. As we left the customs checkpoint, Laura leaned to me and whispered, "Raoul is my hero."

I took my place next to him on the airplane and began to tell him our plans to name a holiday after him, and what a fun day it would be to celebrate. But he had already passed out. ❧

MY LIFE IS GARBAGE

THE GARBAGE TRUCK HAS COME AND GONE. I went out to retrieve my empty can, but my driveway was vacant. Hmm. Wait...no, that looks like my garbage can over there — clear across the street.

The explanation was easy enough to figure out: judging from the giant dent, someone had plowed into my garbage can and knocked it half a block away — an impressive feat, given that it had been in my driveway. It's as if the driver swerved to hit it just so. And there, in a panorama across my neighbor's yard, was a week of my history.

Should I just leave all that stuff there? Pretend I didn't see it? It is garbage after all, so is it really even still mine? Ask any street person: once it's on the curb, it's public property. But I really like my neighbor Sam, and he's a famous historian, so by picking through the gummy clues, he'd have an easy time determining whose crap was all over his yard. I had to clean it up.

So there I was, picking up greasy bits out of the street, from his driveway, his grass, his bushes. "Hey," I wanted to announce to every gawking driver who passed, "I'm not looking for anything. It's already mine, see? No, really, it's..." [sigh.] Never mind.

A bug-coated tub dripped ex-yogurt onto my hand as I picked it up. It was from the wonderful chicken curry recipe I borrowed from my friend Laurie. It had turned out great: creamy, spicy, healthy, and decadently delicious. What a great dinner date.

Then I picked up the empty bottle of Washington State merlot and two take-out deli tubs smeared of pesto and chicken salad, emptied during a long, helpful talk with a trusted friend. My heart warmed. I'm lucky for people like that.

I recoiled at what looked like a dead mouse, but it was only that big gray hairball my cat Romeo had croaked onto my couch a few days ago. I was mad at him at the time, but after contemplating the size of the impressive wad, I realized that cleaning it up was certainly easier than expelling it must have been. I hope he is as sympathetic if I ever cough up a toupee.

I grinned at the sheet of graph paper with a hole cut out of the middle. I'd used my X-Acto knife to create a tiny little note to put inside a tiny little gift, well received.

As if I were leafing through a photo album, I finished gathering up all the miscellaneous bits, stuffing the memories into new garbage bags. I returned to my side of the street, a sagging bundle in each hand. As I reached my trash cans I paused, not quite ready to let go, still holding on by the yellow ties. ❦

SAM-SIZED

I LOVE SHOPPING FOR SUPPLIES at Sam's Club. You can buy a jar of martini olives that is as big as your head. "Sorry," I say with a shrug to the checkout girl as I glance toward my Buick-sized pallet of toilet paper. "I haven't been feeling well."

But the clerks don't even blink. My mountain of miscellany is nothing compared to their average customer, who cannot say no to Big Deal. I watch their consciousness grind to a halt at the Impulse Buy display. "Honey," a guy says while punching numbers into his calculator, "if you figure out the cost-per-Frito, this 100-pound bag is like, half price!"

So off they go, Frito-laden, along with a three-foot-high jar of pickles, a suitcase-sized brick of cheddar, a gross of #2 pencils and a 55-gallon drum of shampoo. If you have ever shopped at Sam's Club, you know this is the truth: they don't have a single express lane, but they have four aisles marked "Flatbed Only."

You can't even get through the snack food section for all the people who are staring gape-eyed at a human-sized bag of M&Ms, as if they just met the love of their lives. They freeze. Time stands still. They feel the rush. Violins sing. They wrap their arms around it, take it home lovingly, crawl into bed with it.

Everything is oversized. The room, the lanes, the carts, the people.

I picked up what I needed to stock my bar, feeling a little smug that I was successful in sticking to my list. Almost successful, anyway: I did buy a 25-pound jar of cashews. But c'mon, it was only ten bucks! ❦

GET MY HEAD EXAMINED

I'M INTO ASTROLOGY. And palm reading. Tarot too. Really, I'm into anything I can use to learn about myself without doing any actual introspection.

I'm a Pisces, which basically means I'm a creative drunk who thinks he knows you better than you do. Unfortunately, the gift of intuition does not help a Pisces to understand himself.

Lines on my palm reveal that I will have kids (been there), big job changes (done that), and will live as long as a battleship (I'll get back to you on that). Two palm readers both said I will have three kids, which is unsettling since at last count I only found two.

Phrenology — having the outside of one's head examined — reveals that I am very, very clumsy. That's a no-brainer (the conclusion, not my head). I could have learned the same thing by having my shins examined.

I'm not opposed to introspection. Indeed, I just spent a small fortune on metaphysical psychotherapy. My therapist recently suggested that my body might be inhabited by unwelcome aliens. That feels about right to me.

My problem is that therapists charge $120 per hour to say, "So — what do *you* think about that?" For the price of a lunch my friend Laurie will come right out and tell me what *she* thinks, and she won't waste time on my opinion.

I just read a very interesting article about birth order. I already knew that as a Youngest Child, I was destined to be a silly attention hog. (You're reading this, so you knew that.) But psychologists are digging deeper. Dr. William Ickes found that a boy who has older sisters is more at ease with new female acquaintances than boys who don't. Excellent! I have two older sisters, so I immediately wrote them a thank-you note.

In the very next paragraph I read that men with two older *brothers* are twice as likely to be gay. I have two older brothers. So now that I'm more likely to get along great with women, I'm less likely to care.

The researchers explain the phenomenon this way: a mother's body reacts to her unborn son as if it were a parasite. (Prophetic?) This reaction grows stronger with each birth. (Experience?) To protect itself, the mother's body begins to reject the implanted male as if it were a sandburr. To protect himself, the male parasite learns to act more girly, to disguise itself and placate the host belly. It's survival of the flittiest. The meek really shall inherit the Earth.

Why didn't my fortune-teller see that in the cards?   ❦

PASTA COMA

I HAVE A CHARMING FRIEND who, for no special reason, I only see over lunch. Because we hardly ever cross paths anywhere else, we feel free to tell the truth about everything in our lives. It's liberating, it's honest, and it's ugly.

Last time we met at our usual Italian restaurant, I ordered penne with marsala sauce. She got ravioli, the same thing she always gets. We sat outside on their nice little fake wood patio. The sun was warm, time slowed down, and the mental justifcations began. *Do you want dessert? Oh, no, really I shouldn't, I'm stuffed, but that black chocolate truffle looks great, I should get back to work, but oh why not we'll get two forks and just share it and what's one more glass of wine and boy I don't want to go to back to work neither do I let's order another bottle...*

The meal took the fight out of us. All we wanted to do was sit there and drink. I began to wonder: would pasta have the same effect on hardened criminals? If Scott Peterson had had a fat plate of spaghetti for lunch, I bet he would have skipped carrying his bloody mattress three blocks to a dumpster, much less lugging his dead pregnant wife all the way to the middle of San Francisco Bay. He'd still be droopy-eyed in front of the TV, watching Oprah, dreaming of medical school.

Saddam Hussein, right this minute, would be at the corner cafe with biscotti crumbs in his beard and espresso drips on his belly.

OJ never would have jumped that fence, and he'd have an extra pair of nice gloves.

Road rage? A thing of the past, because you'd miss the lunch hour rush altogether, getting back to work about 3pm, peaceful as Gandhi.

High-carb diet? Maybe it is. But we're saving lives here.

Of course if you're on the Atkins diet and you can't eat pasta at all, throwing your life away like that, then there's nothing I can say to help.

Think about it this way: it costs $120,000 per year to imprison someone. A plate of spaghetti a day would cost about $1,460 per year — a hundredth as much. With the tax money saved by sedating criminals with rigatoni, we could improve education, provide health care, or bomb some oil-producing nation. That is, if we had the energy. ❦

BRACE YOURSELF

WHEN I WAS LITTLE I HAD TO WALK to the dentist by myself. The three blocks felt like the Trail of Tears.

Dr. Hamilton had what I now know to be Parkinson's disease. Then I just called it the shakes. I was ten when I last visited him, sent alone to have four of my favorite molars pulled with pliers out of my head to make way for upcoming braces. As he came at me with a needle of Novocain, his hand quivered left to right, and I began trying to move my head left to right, hoping to align my movements so that his needle would end up in my gums and not my lip. I was too young and shy to cry for help, and no nurse was in the room to intervene on my behalf. A year later, when my mom told me that old man Hamilton had passed away, I replied, "Oh, that's too bad," but what I meant was, *"Finally!"*

Dr. Hamilton was still warm in the ground when the orthodontist got her turn at me. My dad got along well with Dr. Doris because, like him, she was a sailor, and, like him, she had thick, hairy arms and fingers which were scratchy and tasted of tobacco. Her abuses were more meticulously controlled. She lassoed my wildly independent teeth together so tightly my eyes crossed. If I had had any secrets, I would have spilled them.

One hot summer afternoon as I was chewing on an ice cube, the wire of my braces broke. I had been warned not to chew ice, because this very thing could happen. I was afraid to tell my parents, so I just shuffled on my own straight to the orthodontist's office as if to the gallows. She rewired me as one might weave a basket, with tight-tight-tight little yanks, retaliating for my careless defiance by rearranging my teeth seemingly all at once. Fat, stubbly knuckles gripped ape-like around the pliers, and her tightening tugs lifted my head clean off the reclining chair's headrest: "Don't [bounce!] chew [bounce!] ice [bounce!] ever [bounce!] again!"

I didn't.

All this came back to me last night.

A motley crew had been assembled to become our first company softball team. We were at best rusty, at worst just plain incompetent. Most every ball thrown at me was a little wild and low, skipping unpredictably off the gravelly infield. I played first base, so a lot of wild balls were thrown at me. This meant I must either (1) lower my glove and try to guess where the next bounce would end up, or; (2) jump out of the way, squealing like a sissy.

Along with my dad's curvaceous nose and leathery hands, I inherited his raw shins. There is absolutely no meat in front of the bone. If you feel them, you can sense every woodgrain-like nuance of my tibia. It is as educational as the see-through plastic human model we had in biology class. My dad was a strong, stocky man, so the skinny leg effect looked unsettlingly like Big Bird.

In my years I've learned that a softball to the shins makes the same sound as the crack of a wooden bat. But as wincingly convincing as that is, and as vulnerable and tender as my exposed shins are, whenever a ball came bouncing at me, my glove instinctively ended up in front of my mouth. ❦

FEVERISH

IT HAPPENS EVERY YEAR IN NEBRASKA. In mere days we go from a foot of snow to *Spr-r-ring!* sung with a rolling *rrr* and a lilt in the voice. I become useless, staring through the window like a starving man in front of a Godiva store.

When I have spring fever I make herculean efforts to avoid my job, even resorting to doing other work instead. This morning as I ascended the stairs that constitute a commute from Home to my attic Office, I paused to analyze the little cat footprints left on my newly varnished steps.

My friends suspect my cats are dead. They never move unless I have something they can eat, scratch up, puke on or otherwise befoul. It is their job, and they commit to it day and night.

I live in an old house. The task of refinishing the lovely wooden steps on my staircase took three weeks longer than the single week I had planned. The carpet came off, and left a dusty, gritty layer of dirt and bio-chaff representing the fifty year DNA history of the previous owners. Underneath I discovered that a previous handyman had tried to silence the squeaky steps with a few nails, then a few more, then bigger ones, then in an obvious blaze of frustration, about two hundred fat, flat-head nails cratered in well beyond the stair surface. The stairs still squeak.

I puttied the holes and used a stain pen to try to draw the wood back on. From far away, in the dark, it looks great.

The final step, varnishing, was at hand. I've shared living arrangements with cats for twenty years, so I knew to build a big barricade out of cardboard to keep them off of the sticky new finish. Humans wouldn't want gummy, smelly varnish on their feet. For cats, going where they are forbidden is their life's mission.

Cat Spekky is a hair factory. Just blow a puff of air across her back and fur will fly off like dandelion seeds. She had been sleeping in the sun all day, but her cat-radar alerted her something was now off-limits. Her eyes popped awake, ans she immediately began lurking nearby, analyzing the cardboard barrier to find its weak spot. You could see it through her thin disguise of indifference. "Go on, I'm just admiring your work," her half-opened eyes said comfortingly. "Everything's fine. Feel free to leave the room for just one minute..." I know that look, so I made my barrier stronger and taller, and triple-duck-taped it to the wall.

While simultaneously building my Great Wall and keeping a wary eye on the scheming feline, I had forgotten to keep track of my other cat, Romeo, a giant hairy Maine Coon famous for his ability to tease out black chunks of matted fur as big as apples. He doesn't shed; he harvests. I didn't notice that he had already gone upstairs, so instead of barricading him out of the varnished area, I had sealed him in.

[sigh.]

Nonetheless, the footprints were cute. I traced his path as he meandered down the wet steps, inspected the wall, wandered back up, then back down again, circling around a bit before attempting to jump the wall altogether. He never remembers that he had been declawed, so there were lots of skid marks.

I thought about leaving the prints in the varnish, like those little plaster casts of your hands you made as a kid, on the presumption that your parents would cherish one more handprint on something.

I was supposed to be going to work. This could wait until later, but it was spring and I didn't feel like doing my real job and this wasn't really work at all and I thought heck-it'll-only-take-a-minute, and I spent the next two hours with a palm sander buffing the hairy prints out the steps.

I made it to work about lunchtime. Normally I think it is luxurious to have big windows in front of me while I'm working, but that spring day I just kept staring at my basketball hoop. It looked lonely. I felt guilty, as if I had abandoned it in exchange for adulthood. Worse, it was bill-paying day. The longer I put it off, the longer I would have money.

Soon, every day will be seventy degrees, and we will start taking them for granted. But on the first calm spring day in Nebraska, when the sun bastes freshly exposed skin until it tastes hot and salty, I want to just sit, mesmerized by the parade of pink bellies and freckling shoulders and shiny white shins as they greet the new sun like cicadas crawling out of the mud. Midwesterners are beautiful that way, something that people in Palo Alto will never understand. 🐾

GOD'S DENTIST

MY DRIVEWAY IS STEAMING. The chilly morning rain is drying before my eyes. Just last Monday I was chopping ice off my my back steps. Now I'm all excited to quit work a little early and shoot hoops in the warming sun. Then I remember — *shit!* I have a dentist appointment at 4:30pm.

Just this morning I was giddy about the prospect of promised springtime thunderstorms, the first of the season, and the blizzard which had been forecast to follow on the weekend. Nothing in life tastes sweeter than pancakes and a cappuccino while watching my neighbor shovel snow on a Sunday morning. But God is pre-emptively balancing my karma by giving the rest of the world this glorious, sunny day while I lie flat on my back in a squeaky vinyl dentist's chair, all ten fat fingers of the frustrated former football player wedged into my mouth.

With my dry, cracking lips about to tear apart to accommodate his meaty mitts, he'll say, "How's business?" I don't even pretend to converse anymore. I just concentrate all my thoughts into one watery-eyed glare. "Fuck off," I say, but it comers out "Mpphrlf." He goes in deeper, up to his elbows. "Good, good — glad to hear it."

My dentist is very religious. He plays exclusively Christian radio in his office, which I believe is his way of making me grateful for the sound of the drill. I search the eyes of his staff for any sign of mutual irritation, hoping for an ally to help me foment a radio rebellion. But their souls are lost, the Stepford Assistants.

"I see you've been grinding your teeth."

"Well, yeah," I think to myself, "it's your fucking radio station."

God knows I'm not going to come out against Christian music, what with Him being in charge of lightning and all. It's the music this station chooses to broadcast. Why is it all so awful? I used to belong to a Baptist church, so I know firsthand that there are endless hours of great religious music. Sing anything out of a Baptist hymnal and you'll want to rise up, puff out your chest, march around the room and impose yourself on a heathen.

Catholic Christian Christopher Columbus brought back coffee and chocolate from the Caribbean for Queen Isabella. Why in the world didn't he bring back their music? "Izzie! Check out these moves I picked up in the Americas!" Just like that, church music would have sounded less like Sousa and more like samba.

Lately I have been hanging out with Presbyterians, whose music is mostly of German origin and sounds like it was written by dutiful people who never sleep late on Sunday mornings, which they are.

I'm certain that God does not prefer bland music. God is not subtle. He cuts lakes in half, turns people into pillars of salt and sets bushes on fire. His weather every day is a brilliant display of fireworks and extremes. (Unless you live in helplessly homogeneous San Diego, where right now, I can tell you without looking up, it is 73 degrees.)

God is not subtle about his sense of irony either, giving me this first-of-the-year bright spring day when I have to go to the dentist. My appointment is looming, and just the thought of dusty latex digits worming into my mouth is making black clouds gather over my head.

Would it be rude to bring earplugs? 🦌

WAR GAMES

LOOKING THROUGH MY CLOSET, I discovered a stash of old board games I still have around. Seeing them as an adult, I wondered no longer how the world got so screwed up.

Thoughtful observers finger the influence of violent video games, which train our children to shoot first and look later, to steal a car and drive over someone's perfectly good yard or perfectly good sister.

But my childhood games weren't the paragon of propriety, either. I was raised on this:

Tuba-Ruba: this is the game that requires young boys and girls to be wrapped together in plastic tube bondage, where they slither and writhe against each other trying to coax balls along the tube. It's like full-contact Twister, ages three to twelve.

Twister? Well, wink-wink, nudge-nudge, socially acceptable intertwining. It's supposed to be sexy, but for me it was mostly my older brother's butt in my face.

Mousetrap employs all sorts of shoving, slapping and kicking apparatuses, and you can't win until you master using a bowling ball to knock an old man head first into an empty barrel.

Ouija Board: I can't believe I was given a game centered entirely around summoning the dead. Nice, Mom.

The rest of the games all involved some sort of destruction, deception, or other mercenary behavior among friends. *Battleship:* drop bombs blindly until your opponent has nothing left for you to take potshots at. *Monopoly:* you win when nobody else can afford a place to live. *Risk:* kill everyone with a roll of the dice, and the world is yours. "Hey, kids — let's declare a war!"

True, our children devote hours to video games where they practice stealing cars, kicking cops off their motorcycles and shooting whatever pops out from the corner. Coincidentally, I notice every actual car accident was a chase or a hit-and-run. It's the new instinct: just keep moving and don't look back.

I found my old set of jacks the other day, tucked in a little black leather pouch laced at the top. I tossed them into my travel bag, hoping to scatter them out during long airport layovers. I imagined sitting cross-legged on the floor, squeezing that familiar red spongy ball back to a friendlier place, where terms like *tensies, chicken-in-a-basket* and *'round-the-world* were considered tough talk. But the airline security officer confiscated my jacks — they were too dangerous. ❦

HEART BEAT

VALENTINE'S DAY IS THE MOST STRESSFUL of holidays, if you ask my male friends. Maybe less so for women, because most women are convinced they have a God-given gift of gift-giving. They actually *like* to shop. Men, who are perfectly willing to cheerfully invade another country, are terrified of Valentine shopping because, no matter what they do, it will be a bomb.

He can't buy her a gift card just to get it over with. "Oh," she'll say, "I see how much you care!" And she'll cry. Or if she's the type, she'll bottle it up and then start crying sometime in August, and when he asks her what's wrong, she'll bark, "Nothing."

"But it cost fifty bucks!" he'll reply, baffled. Dollar value makes sense to guys. No gift has a plainer value than a gift card. A $5 card is five times more meaningful to a guy than a $1 card. Buy a guy a $50 gift card and watch the commitment flags pop up around his head like spring dandelions.

Yet a guy doesn't judge a woman by her gifts. If it's a great present, he'll say "Wow! Cool!" He'll put it on the mantle. If it's a stupid present, he'll say "Wow. Cool." He'll put it in the basement. He'll forget in a week who bought him either one. He won't burst into tears and say, "I can't believe you didn't give me an engagement ring!" Right now in my basement I have four coffee cups with slogans imprinted on them, a rubber-band six-shooter pistol, a glass paperweight with a dead fish in it, and a George Bush bobble-head doll.

Years ago for Valentine's Day I once presented a girlfriend with an interchangeable-head screwdriver. I thought it was romantic since I didn't buy one for myself too — that seemed to make it more special. But I got The Look: chin lowered, eyes dead as a snake's. She hissed without a blink, "Girls don't screwdrive."

"But look!" I replied with genuine enthusiasm, thinking maybe she didn't get it. "It ratchets!" [Enthusiastic demo of ratcheting.] "See?" [Ratchet-ratchet-ratchet...ratchet...pop out #8 Phillips head, pop in #6 hex head...ratchet...ratchet... ratchet...]

[sigh.]

After presenting a five-minute dissertation entitled *How Men Don't Have the Sense To Choose a Meaningful Present,* she gave me a heart-shaped jar of rose-scented bath beads. I am six-feet-two, and I have not fit in a bathtub since I was eight.

"Wow. Cool." Basement.

Women *do* judge you by your presents, and they are hangin' judges. "Chocolates!? I can't believe you got me *chocolates!* You *know* I've been on a diet since New Year's Day!" (Cries.) Buy her a membership to the gym: "You think I'm fat!" (Cries.) Give her a gift card: "Amy's boyfriend bought her chocolates!" (Cries.)

Women are wrap artists. They own clear plastic tubs filled with endless colorful wrapping papers, ribbons and tape. Men can design a stealth bomber with a pencil and napkin, but they can't tie a bow. When those pretty foil gift bags were invented, we thought salvation from the agony of gift-wrapping had come, but women took one look at the pretty sack and knew we just got it over with.

So, my friend asked my advice. "What *do* you get a woman for Valentine's Day?"

"Do something sentimental," I suggested. "Give her something that you make yourself. It has to take at least an hour, or she'll think you made it up at the last minute because you forgot it was Valentine's Day, which you did." I thought of my past successes and failures. "But if it takes you more than two hours to make, she'll think you're a stalker and file a protection order."

If you are buying a gift for a guy, go ahead and get a ratcheting multi-headed screwdriver. But you may never know whether he likes a tool-type gift because, either way, he'll say "Wow! Cool." and put it in the basement.

Above all, keep this fact in mind: you are taking advice from a single guy. ❦

CHING-CHING!

TANDEM BICYCLES WERE EVERYWHERE when I was a kid. It must have been a fad because I hardly ever see one now. We didn't own one, but I remember riding one all the time. I think we just took one from the neighbor's house. When you are a kid, the world is communist.

In a fit of nostalgia I decided it would be fun to find an old tandem bicycle and fix it up with bright paint and streamers and a horn, all Pee-Wee Herman-like. When it comes to dorkiness, I am gifted.

I searched online. I learned right away that e-Bay is for people who can't say no. I think people would buy cow shit just to keep someone else from buying it first. Posted by an Iowa farmer, I found a photo of a Schwinn tandem bicycle. The picture was taken in a field, buffalo grass growing up through the bike's rusted frame. It was not a classic bike. It was barely a bike at all. Price: $500. He did not smile when I asked whether the property came with it.

I took out a want ad in the newspaper, figuring every fifth garage had an abandoned tandem hanging from the rafters. I got a dozen calls, all from people who had first checked e-Bay to see what their bike might be worth. "I have a 1978 Columbia," my first caller said. "It's a classic. We want $350 for it. It's all original, except it's broken in half and we lost the back half, and we can't find the front tire."

"So," I replied, "it's basically a hoe with handlebars?"

I eventually visited a nice couple in Omaha's perfectly sensible Keystone neighborhood. In their driveway leaned a former majestic beauty, all curvy lines and wide, spring-loaded seats, as creamy white as Barbie's purse. The fenders were off and she had knobby dirt tires where old-school whitewalls should have been, but at least she had tires. "Is $40 too much?" he asked with a shrug.

Sold.

The bike was so long and heavy that it was easier to put my truck on top of it rather than the other way around. I had a bike rack, the kind that hangs off the spare tire on the back of my truck, but the bike was so long it stuck out across three lanes. It took three of us to heft her onto the roof rack, where she sagged like a mattress, but we got her home.

We tried to test-drive her. I have never had so many near-death experiences in a single city block. She is definitely a downhill bike: 1) she is too heavy to go uphill, and, 2) the brakes don't work.

I fell in love. I named her Daisy.

I quickly reduced Daisy to a box of ball bearings, greasy cables, sprockets and frame tubes. Hanging her frame from the ceiling, I spray-painted her powder blue, along with half my basement. I scoured the Earth to find whitewall tires and finally succeeded, but they turned out to be one hundredth of an inch bigger than the original fenders would hold, so the wheels couldn't turn. On the Internet, there is a store for everything, and I found fenders too, fat, flared and chrome.

So far I have spend $450 on my $40 bike. But she is gorgeous, with pearly tassels spewing from the grips, and a handlebar basket calling out for a baguette and bottle of wine. She even has a ching-ching bell and a squeeze-bulb horn, which I bet is the root of the word *honkey*. After her inaugural ride she has rested in the basement. No amount of enthusiasm or money will make her easier to pedal, and eventually I'll have to go uphill.

Neighbors still talk of seeing me coming down the hill, streamers flying, bell ching-chinging, teeth bared, pie-eyed, legs flailing, screaming for clearance. This wasn't exactly how I imagined it. ❦

CANDY, LITTLE GIRL?

DOES ANYONE KNOW WHY, when a plane is going to crash, the pilot is supposed to yell into his radio, "Mayday! Mayday!"? Wouldn't it make more sense to yell "Crashing?" Or scream, "Holy-Sweet-Mother-Of-All-Things-That-Fly..." I think it's a mistake to expect a guy to remember a random code word while he's wetting his pants. "Easter! No, wait — Labor Day? Dang, what was it? Oh yeah — Mayday! Mayday!"

"Crashing!" At least the control tower guys would know right away that you have a problem. Yell "Mayday" and they're likely to check the calendar. "Wow, Jim, is it May Day already? I need to go get Margaret a basket. I forgot last year, you know, and never heard the end of it."

I'm writing this on May Day. I don't sense a commitment to the holiday so much these days, but when I was a kid we commited time and resources to making May baskets. The rules were thus: you leave a May basket at the door, ring the bell, and run away. The recipient is expected to run you down and try to kiss you, so be sure you have the right address.

May Day is a cross between Halloween, Tag, and Spin the Bottle. I was a fast and competitive kid, so to me it was all about outrunning someone. I didn't get kissed much. I didn't really understand that it was a rite of spring, but I was sissy enough to truly enjoy weaving pink paper baskets and arranging them with colorful candy.

On any other day, if a boy came to the door hoping to kiss my eight-year-old daughter, I'd beat him into a Raisinette. But as a kid on May Day, there I was at the dining table with my mom, forming a tidy square basket with strips of pastel-colored construction paper, staples and tape, listening dutifully to her instructions on how to be chased by girls. "Now remember, Dear," Mom said, "make sure her dad knows it's May Day, so he doesn't whip you."

Try on any other day to run a girl down from behind and tackle her for a kiss. You'll find yourself on the corner of Reform School and Mace. There was the one exception of The Reverend Wells's daughter. I had heard she was fast, even though she ran slow.

May Day is the only event I can think of where you get rewarded for not running your fastest. Zoom more than a block and your pursuer will give up and go back inside. You've won, but you've lost.

I was focused on one special girl. Her name, appropriately enough, was Candy. I went to her door, rang the bell and took off. I looked over my shoulder. Nothing happened. I stopped and waited in the silent street. I crept back, rang again and ran again, a little less enthusiastically this time. No Candy, no anybody. The house was empty.

I checked for witnesses. There were none, so I went back and retrieved the basket. ❦

TERRIBLE WASTE

I INHERITED MY MOTHER'S Depression-born frugality. It nearly killed me recently to throw out an entire quart of milk. I was about to take a big swig but hesitated, maybe due to a magic self-preservation instinct, or maybe only because I remembered the milk had traveled in a camping cooler bouncing in the back of my truck over a seven-hour trip through the Nebraska Sandhills in August. So I took a little swirly test-sip, my eyes shifting left to right as if evaluating a cabernet sauvignon. I felt something solid, and spat.

It wasn't the cooler's fault. There was still ice in it. So I checked the milk carton's expiration date. It had passed two weeks ago. The otherwise nice man at the marina shop had sold me some very aged food. That's fine for cheese, and this milk was well on its way, but still.

My friend Sarah had gone with me to the marina's store, and the donut display gave her a "come hither" look which stole her heart and stopped her mid-stride. I harrumphed with disapproval, and was even more judgmental when she passed up all the great shiny glazed ones, even the waxy black chocolate ones, for some plain old cake donuts. Of course, when we arrived with our booty back at camp, I was the first to open the box, dangle a donut in front of our fellow campers, and bite in. I nearly chipped a tooth.

Apparently the kindly old man running the store had stocked the place once, years ago, and nobody had ever bought anything.

I performed a donut demonstration. I put one under each foot and stood. It was supposed to be funny. I didn't expect them to actually hold me up, but were it not for the imbedded sand and cockleburs I could have put them back in the box.

I revived them back to edibility by soaking them in some strong coffee. Hey, I already paid for them. And after all, they're donuts.

We returned home from the trip and I unpacked my giant plastic food tub and its unfinished remnants, which included a nearly full bag of double-chocolate-chip cookies. The tub also included a cockroach. The itinerant hobo had jumped our train and made the seven hour trip in luxury. As I flicked the bug out the back door, my camp-mate said, "You want me to throw these cookies out — right?"

"Right?" was rhetorical for her. She hadn't met my mom, so she doesn't know my upbringing. As she dangled the nearly full bag of cookies over the garbage like a convicted felon in a noose, my mouth went dry. "Of course, t-t-throw them out," I croaked. "There was a cockroach in there. That'd be gross."

The next day, after a nice, healthy lunch salad, I thought, "man, I really, really want a cookie." Of course I knew right where to find one. From the start they had been calling to me from the garbage can like the Telltale Heart. They're still wrapped in the plastic bag, I reminded myself. And they're still on top of the other garbage, right?

Almost. They weren't quite on top, as it turned out. I found them under two clumps of wet coffee grounds, a J. Crew magazine, three days of mail, and two bags of scooped cat litter. But hey — the cookies were still wrapped in plastic. Right?

I ate four, accompanied by a demitasse of steaming espresso. The cookies were still pretty crunchy, which is impressive because garbage cans are often humid. The unsettling thing was that it tasted slightly of banana. Banana and chocolate go well together — that's not the problem. It's that I remembered there was a banana in the food tub. I tried not to think of that the little hobo cockroach tearing into the banana first, then tracking little roachy banana footprints all over my chocolate cookies.

I know she saw the look of anguish in my eye as those cookies were suspended like purgatory over the rest of the garbage, and perhaps she knew all along that I'd dig them back out after she left.

But they were wrapped in plastic. Right?

I called my mom. I didn't say anything about the cookies. I just missed her, and wanted to hear the voice of someone who would understand. 🍎

POTTY TRAINING

I OWNED A BAR CALLED MICK'S, and it had the smallest bathrooms ever. That's the legacy of old buildings, grandfathered from the generous new laws designed to protect and accommodate the excremental rights of people in wheelchairs.

Here is how small the bathrooms are: if you were to practice your bow-and-arrow skills in it, you would hang your target on one end of the room, walk to the other end, draw your bow back until your elbow bumped the door, then as you released your arrow it would not have pulled away from the string before it began piercing the bulls-eye. Even the nerdy kid picked last for the archery team would get a perfect score, unless he completely lost control of the bow and shot the arrow up his nose.

If I hung a basketball hoop in the bathroom, a jump shot would scrape knuckles across the ceiling. You wouldn't so much shoot the ball as just lean over and drop in through the hoop.

I pondered these sports analogies as I cleaned the bathroom at the end of the night. (This is a job one can expect with a dual degree in psychology and philosophy.) My bathroom had been used by the very same guys who leap to their feet and shriek at the television in disapproval when an eighteen-year-old freshman quarterback in his first televised game misses a 40-yard pass attempt to a receiver running cross-field, full-bore in double-coverage, while the quarterback was scrambling to escape five 300-pound, armor-clad, spit-slinging ape-men. These same squealing sports fans — not from ten paces, not from one pace, but from six inches — cannot hit the urinal: a big, wrap-around target you nearly touch with the barrel of your little skin pistol that you've been toting your whole life.

If our paper towel dispenser fell off the wall, the whole thing would drop straight into the trash can without touching the rim. That is to say, throwing away your used towels is not a hard shot. Yet about ten wet towel attempts a night will bounce onto the floor, and stay there, unrebounded. It's not like the next guy in line for the toilet lunged in to deflect the shot-on-goal. After watching six straight hours of basketball, what guy can't hit the opening of a trash can that is practically between his legs?

The strangest inconsistency with men's bathroom behavior is the jolt of horror when a guy opens the one-man-bathroom door and discovers someone is already in there. From the panic spasm you'd think he had stumbled upon his parents entangled in a naked embrace. He recoils, turns his head, slams the door. Yet on a football field this same shy quarterback doesn't think twice about sliding his rough, confident hands high between the thighs of the squatting center, who eagerly offers the big leathery ball between his legs, all this right in front of a few thousand onlookers.

So perhaps the answer to lazy bathroom behavior is to have men pee in front of a crowd, giving them points for accuracy. "He's coming up to the wall now...he's in his stance...he let's it fly...*score!* ❦

PLAYING WITH STRANGERS

WE ARE SUPPOSED TO GET SMARTER as we get older.

A friend and I discussed how, when we were little, we could just walk up to a kid we didn't know and say, "Do you want to play?" And then we'd play. It didn't matter if the kid looked different, was cute or was a complete booger-face. You didn't judge him — you just said, as plain as the boogers on his face, "You have boogers on your face." The kid wouldn't get mad — he'd just say "Oh," wipe them off with his mitten, and then you'd play.

To play with a kid you didn't know, you didn't have to say, "Hi, fella, can I buy you a soda?" or make a clever come-on line. Nobody ever gave you a belittling brush-off. "Sorry, I'm looking to play with someone farther up the food chain." Or, "Sure, I'd love to. How about the 4th of Never? Does that work for you?" If playing didn't go well and the kid turned out to be a little jerk, you just quit and told your mom, which is still a pretty good system.

A few weeks ago I went to see a movie and the only seats left were in the front row. I could nearly touch the screen with my toes. I cursed.

I thought about asking for my money back, but I knew that never works. As the commercials began, I recalled how I used to beg my mom to let me sit in the front row, because that would be *so cool!* I imagined entertaining the full house with my brilliant shadow puppets, which is probably exactly why my mom never let me sit there. As an adult it didn't even occur to me to make a shadow puppet, which is sad, because I used to haver a pretty good shadow impression of a barking dog, a hopping rabbit, and a lying Richard Nixon.

As a little boy I was a sensitive soul. I built a hotel for cats in the backyard that on any day had a guest roster of at least three strays. Then, without so much as a bolt of lightning, I got a year older and turned into the God of Destruction. I would make a daily trip to the giant elm tree in the back corner of our yard, unzip my pants, whip out my tiny peeing Gatling gun and — *tff-tff-tff-tff-tff* — decimate the carpenter ants bunkered in the hole of the tree. The Exterminator.

I'd spend an hour meticulously setting up army men in my sandbox, careful to avoid the land mines laid beforehand by cats, until each man was perfectly positioned to serve his country, to risk his life conquering the other end of the sandbox. Then in one cataclysmic ambush I'd smash both sides with wide open hands, sand flying, the painstaking, puny war plans no more than a piffle to God.

One Fourth of July I skipped the flying fireworks in favor of tiny explosives that I could drop into cicada holes, killing them as they napped in their living rooms. But I let no one else have that power over my backyard domain: one day a cicada killer, one of those huge wasps with an inbred, single-minded mission, carried off a screaming cicada, hoping to lay eggs in its head. I threw a brick, which with divine guidance squashed the wasp flat against the tree while sparing the stunned cicada. I froze for a second, then became weightless in the delirium of my newfound superpower. I would thereafter see myself as Snow White, a friend to bunnies and squirrels and cats and cicadas, a bane to wasps and snakes and ants.

My benevolence did not extend to humans. As an adult I once nearly died on a deserted stretch of country highway as I swerved my truck to avoid a raccoon. The SUV rocked left and right, as if the tires were stretched to their limits, and I barely managed to avoid a rollover. Yet earlier the same day, when a pedestrian crossed mid-block in front of me, I honked and drifted closer to him than I needed to just to show him how stupid he was, that it was only by my good grace that he was allowed to live.

At nine years old, I watched with morbid interest as my friend Eric readied for his attempt to jump his bicycle off a long row of picnic tables we had assembled end-to-end. It would be cool if he succeeded, cool if he crashed. Eric ran several practice runs down the narrow, elevated runway, sliding ominously on the slick, green painted surface right up to the precipice. He backed up for the last time, goosed it for keeps, and in noiseless slow-motion he flew off, hitting the ground back wheel first in a rattling *ka-klunk* — a perfect landing. I was impressed, and disappointed.

Another boy, some kid we didn't know, was inspired to copy the feat. We gave him room while he made the same serious test runs, but on the third test he went a little too fast, too far for the glossy tabletops. He nearly stopped in time, but in the slowest possible motion, his front tire slipped over the edge, and his bike began to nose downward. It paused as the mid-bike sprocket teeth tore into the edge of the table, rolling him further towards perpendicular, then *teeeeeetering* over the edge until he and his bike nose-dived into a wad on the hard ground, his crotch smashing onto the chrome gooseneck of the handlebars. Only boys know this specific pain. I watched him as he crawled on his hands and knees all the way out of the park, all the way home, leaving his bike in a twisted tangle in the grass. It must have hurt bad — no kid leaves his bike.

The show was over. Eric shrugged. I went home. ❦

ARE YOU MY DAD?

MY DAD LOOKED A LOT like Walter Cronkite. Dad and Walter both smoked. Both wore black horn-rimmed glasses and started out with buzz-cuts, then in the 1970s grew their hair out a bit. They both had an air of calm, kindly authority. They both liked sailing. I figured all old guys were like that.

My Dad looked like Captain Kangaroo too. I became suspicious when I realized I only saw the Captain in the morning, and Mr. Cronkite at night. I had already discovered that the guy who hosted *Creature Feature* late on Saturday night was also a newscaster on the same station at noon, so it wouldn't be the first time a TV personality was caught moonlighting.

Walter Cronkite was nicknamed "The Most Trusted Man on Earth." To me, so was Dad. Captain Kangaroo was the kindest man on television besides Mr. Rogers, but I didn't really trust him, any more than I trusted Bozo the Clown. Both gave me the creeps. When I mentioned this to a friend, she told me she got the creeps from the Captain's sidekick, Mr. Green Jeans, whom she thought was a pedophile. None of us had reason for any of these feelings, and it's nothing that a good psychologist couldn't sort out.

Mr. Green Jeans troubled me only because I confused him with Greensleeves, and to this day whenever I hear the song *What Child Is This?* I think of Captain Kangaroo. I have the same problem with *A Mighty Fortress is Our God* always bringing to mind *Davey and Goliath,* the claymation children's show, but the Martin Luther composition really *was* Davey's theme song, so that's different.

It also bugged me that Mr. Green Jeans wore blue overalls. I think if your job is to be on TV, and your name is Billy Bowtie, you should wear a bow tie.

I liked Mr. Green Jeans well enough, but I couldn't understand how he got a TV job. The show featured a grandfather clock that could talk, a kid who could transform himself into anything in his imagination, a moose who told knock-knock jokes, and Fred, who was basically a kid made of rubber bands. Mr. Green Jeans might occasionally pull a carrot or potato from his pocket, claiming they came from his fields, but that was about it for his schtick. My dad grew carrots and potatoes from scratch and never got on TV for it.

Mr. Green Jeans looked a whole lot like Howdy Doody. Perhaps this is all more than a coincidence: remember Clarabell, the clown on *The Howdy Doody Show?* The clown was originally played by: guess who? Captain Kangaroo, who was fired from the clown job for being a rabble-rouser behind the scenes. You'd think this is all going to weave together into one cohesive, remarkable pattern, but it isn't.

Today, creepy is normal. There are no fatherly look-alikes. On *South Park,* the children on the show sing a little ditty about Cartman's mom being a dirty whore. In comparison, the foulest villain on *Captain Kangaroo* sang this theme song:

> *My name is Crabby Appleton*
> *I'm rotten to the core*
> *I do a bad deed every day*
> *And sometimes three or four*

Now how can you stay crabby with a theme song like that?

There, I finally see, is the difference between my dad and Walter Cronkite, between my dad and Captain Kangaroo, Mr. Rogers, even Crabby Appleton: my dad never had a theme song. 🍎

COLD WORLD

WHEN I WAS A KID, people came to your door to sell you things. This worked well for years here in Nebraska, because Midwesterners have a hard time being rude right to your face, especially if you're wearing that long, forlorn face door-to-door salesmen are so good at, like the little flower guy who walks up to your table while you're on a date and tries to sell you roses. How do you say "fuck off" to that beagle-faced sad-sack with the droopy eyes, in front of the girl you're trying to impress?

These days most salespeople sit on their anonymous butts, sipping cheap coffee, loading up for their over-caffeinated, spitty, talk-so-fast-so-you-can't-interrupt-them sales pitch over the phone. And I find, in spite of my mother's best efforts, I like being rude in return.

This morning a Mr. Neibaum called. He had "a c-c-commodities offer," he stammered. Then he asked, "Can I call you in February? Does that sound okay with you?"

"Wait," I said, "do you mean to say you called me to ask if you can have permission to call me?"

"Well — I...I have these c-c-commodities. Do you know what commodities are?" Telemarketers have elaborate scripts with little tabs on the pages so they can turn to the right response page for just about anything you might say. You could hear him flipping pages.

"Sure, I know what commodities are," I said. "What I don't know is why you would call a stranger to ask permission to call him."

"Have you ever heard of cold-calling?" It was his first sentence without his nervous stutter, so I figured he had given up on his script for good and was speaking from the heart. Already I liked him better.

"Yes, I've heard of cold-calling," I responded. "I've heard it doesn't work very well because no one ever buys anything from cold-callers, and it's horribly demeaning and demoralizing for the caller. They say callers often feel as if they're selling out their souls. Many even end up committing suicide. Do you feel sad and demoralized, Mr. Neibaum?"

I took his long silence for a yes. "Now, Mr. Neibaum," I continued, "just for today I'm willing to offer you my best-selling report, *How To Feel Better About Yourself and Not Bug People First Thing in The Morning,* for only $39.99. That's 60% off the regular retail price, Mr. Neibaum — I hope you understand this is a one-time discount just because I know you. Would you prefer to pay cash or charge?"

It was a solid close, I thought, but I pushed too far. "Of course, we don't accept checks from telemarketers."

I blew it. Never insult a customer, no matter how dearly you want to. Comments that translate into "Sorry, but we suspect you are an underfunded deadbeat," or "Do you know what commodities are?" offend your mark and spoil your sale. I heard Mr. Neibaum hang up with a lifeless, flaccid *click*...

I paused, listening carefully to hear a distant gunshot.   ❧

ARE YOU GOING TO EAT THAT?

Vegemite is a slimy sandwich spread made from yeast scraped off the bottom of beer vats. Australians are raised on it; nobody else will go near it. It is what Aussies crave most when they travel abroad.

When I first went to visit my little sister in Madrid, I discovered that Americans have their own Vegemite: peanut butter. It cannot be found anywhere in Spain — not because they haven't discovered it, but because they *have*. It disgusts them. She begged me to smuggle jarloads of it to her.

Smugglers in Europe could hide things inside peanut butter. The smell of it so offends European customs officials that they will avoid opening the jar to peer inside. But thanks to today's tighter airline security, they have to give peanut butter special scrutiny, which they enjoy about as much as a cavity search. It is just one more reason for them to hate Americans.

It was my first trip to Spain. I was already nervous about customs. "Is this really smuggleworthy?" I asked. "If I end up in jail over a jar of peanut butter..." But Sis convinced me with an effective mix of pleading and threats. I stuffed three jars deep into my pile of underwear. It seemed like the safest place.

My friend Raoul reports that the French do not cherish American cheese the way we love their brie. They say "American cheese" with the same sniff that they use when they say "American" in general. The French are aghast that we might eat the orange brick of foodlike product, which they believe is wrapped in foil not to keep germs out but to keep the cheese in. And precisely because Velveeta is wrapped in foil and is the exact shape, color and taste of plastic explosives, it is very iffy to smuggle. Raoul stuffed a brick of it in his young son's backpack. That way, if it were discovered, Raoul figured he could shrug and say, "Aw, that nutty kid — he must have stuck it in there at the last minute! Hawhaw." He arrived in Paris without incident and his eager American friends welcomed him and his brick of cheese as if he had liberated them from Auschwitz.

As it turned out, security didn't even open my bag. Maybe I have a nice face. Maybe it smelled of peanut butter. I was greeted by my sister with the affection one usually gives a doctor bringing a life-saving antidote. "Do you have it?"

"Yes, I had a fine trip, thank you." I handed her the goods.

My brother-in-law, a native *madrileño,* saw it and ran from the room, spitting a screaming string of syllables with the machine-gun rapidity unique to angry Spaniards. The only words I recognized were *americano* and the Spanish words for pig, Madonna and toilet. ❦

CRIMINI!

Monday is a night off for me, so I usually stay home and experiment with some new recipe. I saw a very interesting risotto in a cooking magazine — well, it was a liquor magazine, but still it was a pretty good-looking recipe.

Italian cooking uses a whole raft of unusual stuff, so I spent about $75 on ingredients, including white wine (for the recipe) and red wine (for the cook). It took me a half-hour to round up crimini mushrooms. As it turns out, they are now labeled *bella* mushrooms, because *bella* sells better than *crimini* — which is strange because no Italian recipe calls for *bella* mushrooms. To Italians, all mushrooms are *bella.*

The effort was worth it. I was excited to try something new, and proud of myself for gathering up the ingredients ahead of time. Then I discovered I had forgotten to get the rice. Rice is what risotto *is.* But not just any rice. The recipe specified arborio rice.

Back at the store, I found ten brands of white rice. They had brown rice, long rice, short rice, and — I swear — medium rice. I asked a stock clerk, "Where is the arborio rice?"

"Arborio?" he replied. "Does it come from trees?"

Three stores later, I still can't find it. I call my friend Marco, who is Italian and has made risotto. "Can I substitute regular rice?"

"Well, you *could*," he replied, using the same tone you might expect from someone if you had asked to borrow their underwear. "But that would be weird."

I figured it would be his answer. "I've been to three stores. Where do you get it?"

"Whole Foods has it. It's in the Italian section."

After a fruitless search for the "Italian section," which I suppose was the one with the noodles and Chef Boyardee, an employee told me he found arborio rice among the bulk items, next to the trail mix.

I only bought two cups of it, because that's what the recipe calls for, and it makes enough for six Italians, which is metric, so that equals about four Americans, and I doubt I'll ever make it again after all this.

The cashier: "That's $2.68."

I blinked. I double-checked to make sure I didn't accidentally get the 24-carat gold rice. "It's just rice," I point out. "They pick it out of dirty water."

Whole Foods is not Egypt. Whole Foods does not dicker on price. Her face remained blank as Botox. "It's $2.68."

I grabbed my rice like it was a bag of quarters and left. I was hungry and tired. Of the swear words I reserve for cooking, I had already used up half and hadn't even turned on a burner yet.

Luckily, most Italian food is fun to make. It sits and simmers a long time while you watch and poke and drink wine and stir. By the time the risotto was finally cooked, so was I.

The recipe said to leave the considerable sausage grease in the pan while adding the rice. The rice dutifully soaked up the grease until it looked like little lard beans. When it was done I took an eager taste, and it as light and fluffy as a spoonful of shortening.

The next night I watched my friend Shelley make *coq au vin* in 45 minutes with one hand behind her back, her eyes never leaving the television. Maybe I'll try French cooking next time. ❦

YOU KNOW HU

EVERYBODY WAS MAD. Everybody but me, that is. I like skirmishes — as long as I'm not the one getting skirmished.

Visiting Chinese President Hu Jintao was outraged after a press conference, during which a protester yelled at him to stop killing members of the religious movement Falun Gong. She yelled her protest in both Chinese and English, just so everybody at the media event could get the point, which even the Secret Service said was nice of her. Hu reportedly squealed, "Shoot her! *Shoot.* — uh, I what I mean is, revoke her press pass!"

The host, President George W. Bush, was mad too. He had spent a small fortune of governmens money — and I quote the Associated Press here — "on months of painstaking diplomacy over protocol and staging." In other words, to make sure don't nobody say nuthin' 'bout nuthin.' He later apologized to President Hu. I don't know what form that apology took, but it must have been something like, "I'm sorry she told you to stop killing people."

The Secret Service was mad because the protester, Dr. Wenyi Wang, was no typical rabble-rouser. Dr. Wang, 47, had a government-issued press pass as a reporter for the *Epoch Times*. I think President Bush was probably mad that the Secret Service, in spite of all their "staging diplomacy," didn't catch that *Epoch* is a Falun Gong-affiliated newspaper. "Uh, sorry, boss." Wenyi was removed and later charged with Disorderly Press Comments Not in The Form of a Question. She cannot be charged again for the same offense, because that would be double-Jeopardy.

All this happened after the announcer referred to China as "The Republic of China," which made all the Chinese mad. Mainland China is formally called "The People's Republic of China." That doesn't sound like a big deal to American ears, but The Republic of China is actually the formal name of Taiwan, so it was a bit like introducing George Bush as the President of France.

Worse, China doesn't recognize Taiwan/The Republic of China. A reporter later referred to them as "The Republic of People's China," which offended everybody again, because that is the official name of Tammy and Ken Wang, who are not really recognized by anybody, because they don't go out much. When they do accept an invitation, they never reciprocate. To avoid any further confusion, Hu had Tammy and Ken shot.

Just for Hu's protection, they did not invite the president of the Republic of China, The People's China Republic, nor the Republic of People's China (which we suppose to be defunct now anyway, due to lack of anybody in it).

If you have anything to say to you-know-Hu, be careful to put it in the form of a question. You know how some people get. 🐦

NUTS

LAST TIME SINGER MIKE BUTTERWORTH performed at my bar, he broke his nut. As you can imagine, it threatened to delay the start of his show. He set the broken piece of plastic on the bar and left to go find some glue.

On guitars, nuts are at the top of the neck. If God had given it more than a day's thought, he might have made man the same way. The guitar strings bend over the nut and proceed down the neck to the body. If your nut's broken, you are, of course, out of tune with the world.

Like people, guitars have heads, nuts, necks, heels, shoulders, bottom-decks, waists and sound-holes. Unlike people, those parts appear, from top to bottom, in that order. Like people, guitars have many frets, there is often an electronic pickup line, and — usually — there are strings attached.

The bartender saw the little piece of Mike's nut on the bar and threw it in the garbage. She didn't know — it looked like a broken piece of plastic, which it was. When he returned for it, there was much panicking and trash-sifting. But they rescued the pea-sized chip from the coffee grounds and dirty stumps of lemon wedges. After a big sigh of relief and much congratulating, Mike went back to the stage to get his glue. I passed him with a wave as I walked in to the bar through the stage entrance. As I went to greet the bartender, I noticed a broken piece of plastic on the bar, and tossed it into the garbage. ❧

MAKING YOUR MARK

I THINK IF YOU TRY TO COMMIT SUICIDE by jumping off the Empire State Building, you have a nice sense of romance.

It would be far easier to jump off a parking garage or step in front of a bus. You wouldn't have to take the subway all the way into the city, pay $12 to visit the observation deck and ride all the way to the top, just to fling yourself back to where you started. And that's presuming you live in New York in the first place, and don't have to deal with a 14-day advanced, non-refundable airline ticket. Not to mention that a one-way often costs more.

Those who go through all that trouble want to go out with a little more flair than the average hopeless person. Romantics to the end. They want their name in the *New York Times*.

Imagine you are already feeling like a loser, then this scenario occurs: you step up to the precipice, shut your eyes, say a few words, jump off the top of the Empire State Building, and...and...nothing? Worse than nothing: a giant updraft blows you right back onto the observation deck. You can't even kill yourself right.

That actually happened. Twice. Verified. God only knows how many other times it happened, but people were too embarrassed to admit it.

The Empire State Building recently celebrated its 75th birthday. That's why I'm thinking about it, pondering its unique trivia, such as this: the top of the tower was originally designed as a mooring for dirigibles. (That aforementioned updraft nixed the concept after one terrifying docking attempt.)

The original bid to construct the building included an estimate of one worker death per floor. There are over one hundred floors, but only fifteen workers actually died. So in all, the building was finished forty-five days ahead of schedule, five million dollars and seventy-five lives under budget.

The Empire State Building regained its title as New York City's tallest building after the World Trade Center was knocked down. The Empire itself was once hit by a B-25 bomber, whose American pilot lost his way in thick fog, and parts of that plane punched all the way through the building, raining burning fuel down the other side. Seventy people were killed that Saturday, mostly workers for, of all things, the Catholic War Relief Services. The building reopened for business the following Monday. Engineers said the building was specifically built to withstand exactly such an impact.

Of course there is that whole embarrassing Kong affair. But who could have predicted that? And although Kong definitely had a sense of romance, he didn't jump. He was pushed. ❦

DUCK AND COVER

MY ELEMENTARY SCHOOL had a big red alarm bell on the wall. It wasn't really a bell, I guess, more a big metal bowl screwed to the wall, and a little ball hammer that would beat on it to make it ring. We knew through repititious training that the ringing bell meant:

1) fire,

2) tornado, or

3) Russians

In case of fire, we were taught to walk out very calmly, in single file, which even as kid I knew wasn't going to happen if there were a real fire. I had heard stories of people jumping out of burning buildings to escape flames. If fire could make you jump out a tenth floor window, it certainly would make you cut in line. But I played along dutifully, because we got to go outside.

For alarms (2) and (3) we learned the same procedure: crawl under your desk, curl up in the fetal position and put your hands over your neck. We practiced that too. For (2), I imagined giant beams and bricks pounding down around me in tornadic fury while my mighty metal school desk saved my life. But for (3), I didn't have a clear vision of what a Russian nuclear attack might be like. All I knew of nuclear explosions was from a 1940s-era newsreel I had seen where they tested a bomb in New Mexico, and a little house with a little crash test dummy family blew away straight sideways right out of the camera frame as if they were made of playing cards. So I wondered: should I set my desk on its side? Which way should I face it? In spite of all the practice I didn't feel very well prepared for the Russians.

That triangular nuclear radiation symbol was put on buildings that were supposed to be safe havens against fallout. But then administrators used that same symbol for things that actually were radioactive, so even today if I were to hear that bell go off I wouldn't know whether to run toward the symbol or away from it.

A few days ago I was sitting peacefully on my veranda, enjoying a fine margarita, when heard that distinct bell sound, and loud. It was disorienting because I am no longer a kid and there is no school anywhere near me. All I had at the time for a protective desk was a wobbly folding bistro table and some plastic patio chairs. I couldn't even march around calmly in single file because there was only me.

And then, clear as the bell and just as shrill, I heard bagpipes: real live bagpipes too, not that ubiquitous recording of *Amazing Grace*. It sounded like someone was practicing a few doors down, and that they needed more practice. (Let me interject here that you who practice bagpipes should do it in an appropriate place. Like Antarctica.) The alarm, the bagpipes — were we being attacked by the Irish?

Or was the bell a warning that some Russian fiend was about to play the bagpipes?

Both offending noises continued mercilessly, so I gave up my place on the veranda and its protective wire screens and folding table, and went early to work at my bar. As the clanging and bleating faded behind me, I passed a fully-decorated clown driving, of course, a Volkswagen Beetle. I could tell he wasn't Irish. The Irish aren't that funny.

We exchanged glances. He acted like everything was normal, so I did too.

If I had died as a kid during a Russian attack, I would have left this Earth while cowering under my desk, because I know now that the desk wouldn't have made a bit of difference. Nothing would make any difference. That is a sad way to go. I offer a better plan: if there is an impending nuclear explosion, teachers should hand a lollipop to each student and say, "Good news, kid: school's over early! Go outside and enjoy that bright new sun." ❦

BUT I DATE MYSELF

MEXICANS GREW AGAVE. The Spaniards turned it into tequila. After sampling the result, they both began making human sacrifices to the gods in hopes of a bountiful harvest.

I'm not at all surprised. Tequila gives me visions, if you call that spiritual. I'd pray for more too. That said, I'm not sold yet on having human sacrifices, especially the whole virgin aspect. If anything, I think the gods would be more impressed if you offered up your political leaders than if you whacked some innocent kid, and in the end you'd have more sweet, lovely girls and fewer big fat liars. It's a win-win.

I wouldn't be surprised if most virgin sacrifices came about because the virgin insisted on being a virgin in the first place.

If we do decide to go with human sacrifices, I'd happily make a few nominations.

I've had a messy couple of weeks. I've been kicked at, flirted with, lied to, hugged, fucked off, tease-whizzed, fill-out-this-form-we-will-never-look-at, prove-it, it's-in-the-mail-faxed-Fed-Ex'd-by-snail-what?-

you-never-got-your-important-papers-too-bad-you-have-to-go-to-jail-my-mistake-sorry. Beg your pardon if the governor will give you one.

I was supposed to have a date, who canceled at the last minute. I decided instead to have myself over for dinner.

I started by cutting myself some flowers and offering myself a stiff margarita. "Why, thank you!" I cooked, I ate, I whispered sweet nothings into my own ear. Another margarita? Why, don't mind if I do, but I do believe, sir, that you are lowering my defenses! My lazy smile returned.

I saw lightning bugs, although it was only June. Must be a spiritual vision — fireflies don't usually come out until mid-summer. And the tree across the street was raising its limbs as if to say, "Score!"

Maybe I shouldn't be with me. Maybe I'm not right for myself. But I just can't tear myself away from myself. I'm inseparable. And I don't care who finds out: last night I slept with myself.

I awoke this morning with my arm draped over myself, cute as a bug in my bed. I brushed the silly morning hair sweetly from my eyes, patted myself on the behind and whispered melodically, "Good morning Pumpkin," as I wafted espresso fumes under my nose.

I'm a pretty good date, if I do say so myself. I respected myself in the morning. The best thing is, I'm always there when I need me.

In the morning I noticed the half-empty tequila bottle, and it reminded me: wasn't I going to nominate somebody for something?   ❦

SHOTS

DR. JAY STEWART WAS RECENTLY CHARGED with giving a race horse a shot of vodka. Literally, a shot. Not jigger. Needle. He said it was "to take the edge off." The *Omaha World-Herald* story didn't mention whether the horse was also offered a cigar, but they did specify that it was Phillips vodka, not Grey Goose. I suppose some horses are cheaper dates than others.

Horse trainers (and bettors) say a race can be "lost in the paddocks," which is to say the horse is too wound up before the race, fretting and sweating herself to exhaustion before the gate even opens. One solution is to give the old girl a shot right in the paddocks.

Horse bartending is different from the people kind. Veterinarians pony up as much as a cup of vodka for one shot. I work in a bar. A human shot (jigger, not needle) is one-and-a-half ounces. A strong drink may have double that. There are no classic bar recipes that ask for a cup of vodka. Suffice it to say that our horse had a three-martini lunch right before a race. Take the edge off? Take your legs out.

Apparently, hootching up your horse is not new. Most horse vets have heard of it, though few will admit to doing it. Off the record, I learned that vodka does calm horses, but most vets say it doesn't speed them up. It just gives them confidence. I know what they mean.

Different liquors create different reactions. Injecting a horse with whiskey gives him unwarranted arrogance and makes him mean. Vets avoid giving tequila to horses because it makes them pay more attention to the mares than to the race. After a glass or two of wine, horses shrug and say to each other, "What are we competing for? Let's order in some pizza. Cheers!"

The Nebraska Racing Commission specifies that no drug may be administered which has not been approved by the commission. I don't know whether an appletini, up and with a twist, is approved. But I do know that most people who attend the Kentucky Derby are there only for the mint juleps.

"The injection of alcohol into horseracing is wrong on several counts," the commissioner was quoted, his pun, sadly, not intended. "It impeaches the integrity of the sport by giving a horse an edge."

Now wait a minute — wasn't the original idea of the vodka injections to help take the edge *off?* ❦

SMOKE SIGNALS

CIGARETTE SMOKE SMELLS BETTER when you are outdoors. To me it's paternal incense. My dad was an avid sailor and championship smoker, and my memories of helping him rig his boat include the sweet smell of cigarettes outdoors, Old Spice, and sweat.

And cursing. Dad never once swore at me. Swearing was carefully reserved for challenging, frustrating tasks. It bled off tension. I inherited that gene and continue the tradition to this day, to the dismay of those nearby. "What's the matter?!" they ask upon hearing my *Diatribe to a Stuck Bolt,* or *Ode to A Toilet Gasket.* "Are you okay?"

"Fine...why?" I don't even hear myself do it.

Dad was a considerate smoker. He never flicked a butt into the grass. He never so much as dropped an ash. And yet his mouth was never without a cigarette, the new one ejecting the old stub like a cocked Winchester. He was as machine-like and reliable as the crisp *click!* of a Zippo lighter.

I tried to smoke when I was thirteen. My brother's friend Mike took up the habit, and I thought everything Mike did was cool, because he was two years older and he was not my brother. We would pick a discarded butt from the ashtrays in his house, light the stub, and sucked away dramatically. To cover up our criminal breath, we would crunch into a whole raw onion. Knowing my parents as I do, they were aware all along of my transgression, and figured my cover-up scheme was punishment enough. Dad was a psychologist, so his mind worked that way a lot.

I still think of onions when I need a subterfuge. Just yesterday I grilled them with garlic to hide the lingering smell of fresh cookies I had just baked, so I didn't have to share. Onions: the Liar's Vegetable.

I tried to smoke like Humphrey Bogart, but my dramatic, self-conscious exhales always looked more like Audrey Hepburn. Friends teased me because the dark tobacco stain in my filter was concentrated into a tiny, dense dot in the middle, which they said meant I smoked like a girl. I never did make a connection between the two. But because of the condemnation of my peers and the impossible example of my father, I gave up cigarettes.

I only saw my father cry twice. Once was over a family member who had gotten himself into trouble. The other was in utter frustration with himself, after he had tried to quit smoking for the sake of his family, and failed.

After a lifetime of my dad smoking cigarettes, cigarettes finally smoked my dad.

I have my own sailboat now. I spent last Father's Day on it, thinking of him. I brought along a little Navy boat whistle he had given me, the kind that makes the *oooo-WEEEE* sound you hear in old Navy movies. As I was rigging the boat, I thought about lighting a cigarette. But it just wouldn't have been the same. ❦

THE BIG BANG

I QUIZZED A FEW KIDS about what the connection is between July 4th and fireworks. Not a single kid offered anything about the symbolism of war or the cost of freedom. One did complain about the cost of Red Rats. That's as close as they got. The significance of Independence Day to them is that after a long year of being told to wear a bike helmet and wash your hands and don't run with the scissors, their parents hand them a wad of cash and tell them to go buy an armful of their favorite explosives. "Don't forget punks!"

If you are particular about history, July 4th is a pretty squishy date to celebrate. Independence was actually declared on July 2, 1776. No one signed the document until a month later. It was printed on the 4th, so it was dated the 4th, but that's about all they accomplished that day. When John Adams predicted a "great anniversary Festival...with Pomp and Parade, with Shews, Games, Sports, Guns, Bells, Bonfires and Illuminations from one End of this Continent to the other from this Time forward forever more," he was referring to July 2nd. In the very same letter he expresses his regret that we hadn't "mastered Quebec and been in possession of Canada." Easy there, John.

We have a solid history of celebrating on the wrong day. Some historians believe Jesus was actually born around Easter, although Easter hadn't quite been invented yet, and that Christmas was pasted onto the Winter Solstice just to get the pagans to buy in, since they already had a party planned. We've already moved Lincoln's and Washington's birthdays to an easier-to-party-on date. My friends all agree that Halloween should always fall on a Friday. July 4th can be a holiday just because we say it is. You take a party where you can find one.

During last year's amazing, blazing fireworks display in Omaha, where the *World-Herald* lit a match to $40,000, I pondered the significance of the event. I watched a teenage boy light noisy rockets while his friends and family gathered around so closely that I feared the next missile wouldn't clear their foreheads. This punk with a punk sat with legs astride his projectile, slumped so far over that his nose nearly touched the end of the launch tube. I imagined the rocket snagging his shorts on the way up, carrying his screaming seeds to be scattered across our amber waves of grain.

After every thunderous explosion I expect it to rain fingers. But things work out pretty well every year, and the morning newspaper reports just one or two people who can now only count to seven.

The weather was flawless this year, the fireworks spectacular, the friends hilarious, the wine intoxicating. I felt liberated indeed, and relented to the precept that if a mother wants to provide the means for her fourteen-year-old son to blow off his own testicles — well, go ahead. It's a free country. ❦

THE NAKED TRUTH

My sister Jodi and I were promised by the Italian travel guidebook that if we followed the Cinque Terre Trail, we would come upon a nude beach. With great anticipation we kept our eyes peeled. Thanks to the Internet, I've already seen nearly everyone naked, but I've never seen a naked person in the wild.

We were hiking along a narrow, rocky ridge that followed the Italian coastline high above the Ligurian Sea. It was midafternoon when we finally found the trailhead. There was a tiny wooden sign hidden far enough along the overgrown spur of the trail that it didn't really guide you there as much as it confirmed your guess. It was a perfect secluded, private beach for discreet natural swimmers, and we had a perfectly discreet vantage point to spy on them.

Way down below us we spotted one solitary guy on the beach, pacing around with a mix of optimism and disappointment. He was clearly a tourist too. I suspect that, like us, he had read about the beach in his travel guide. He tried to act casual, like "I do this all the time. I might even be from here." He went for a swim. It was a chilly sixty degrees outside, and judging from the withered consequences either the water was colder or he was Scottish. He put his Speedo on. It sagged.

Nudism is better in the imagination. The newspapers recently reported that private nudist colonies are offering discounted memberships to younger prospects. They say their ranks are aging and membership numbers are flaccid. They report that the median member age is now fifty-five years old.

It is the same problem the Elks Club and the Rotarians have: young people aren't joiners. But I think the problem goes beyond that. Young people also don't want to see old people naked. "Wow, Crystal, isn't that your dad and his bowling buddies over there?"

In addition to the discounted membership, one nudist colony advertised half-price "amenities." What amenities might you need if you are naked? Sunscreen? Duct tape to hold your wallet to your butt? A magnifying glass?

I don't believe nudists when they proclaim that all they want is to "feel free." They're liars — they want to see naked bodies like the rest of us, otherwise they wouldn't care about median member age. If all they wanted was freedom from clothing, they'd walk around naked at home.

There are a few good things about nudist colonies. If you are naked, people are much more likely to notice your expensive new watch, or that flashy engagement ring. And if course, you'll always know when someone is happy to see you. ❦

TOO CLOSE FOR COMFORT

MY NEIGHBOR POISONS RABBITS. You should see her beautiful garden.

I know a guy who carries a gun while he does yardwork. He whips it out whenever he sees a rabbit. He kills over lettuce.

My tomatoes last year were the best ever. At least something good comes from the heat of summer. I do not have a green thumb, and I'm so terribly excited when tomatoes survive to redhood that I give them all away. This year, as each of the early ones was on the verge of pickability, I found they had been munched overnight, still on the vine, looking like a hanging apple core.

Rabbits have never eaten my tomatoes before. I guess I'm flattered. Normally they eat my hostas. The only reason I grow hostas is because I can grow hostas. I wouldn't kill anyone over hostas. Okay, maybe a certain person or two, but that's only because I'm looking for an excuse.

I spend each summer trying to coax rabbits to eat out of my hand. This year one rabbit — Eddie, I call him — came right up to me early in the spring. That was a real breakthrough. Usually it takes all summer, because it goes against every reasonable bunny instinct to risk their lives over a piece of bread. Halfway into the tempting process I was so fascinated by his shiny marble eyes that I didn't notice he had nibbled right up to my finger.

Bunny teeth aren't sharp. They're more like pliers. My flailing and yelping set my training back a few weeks. Eddie has come back, but he gives me a wary look now that says, "Dude — you are unstable."

Yesterday we shared an early morning snack as I told him what was going on in my life. I probably offered too many details, but he listened with long, patient ears. He replied in return that he felt he missed a lot of good things in life because he was always scared of everything.

Then, contradicting himself, he let me touch him.

The only rabbits I've ever petted were those heavy, doped-up California rabbits that sag in your arms as if they just got home from eating a rack of barbecued ribs. They're more like cats. Cats that are high. (Not catnip high — contrary to what I hear all the time, catnip is not "kitty pot." I gave my cats catnip once — the good stuff, too, no ditch catnip — and they got all spun up, irrational and combative. Catnip is not kitty pot. Catnip is kitty meth.)

Eddie didn't feel like a cat. Cats are heavy, meaty and lithe. Eddie was light as a dandelion seed, fragile as a cobweb, so soft I nearly couldn't feel him at all.

Then in a *flit* he bolted, overwhelmed by the danger of getting close to somebody.

I know the feeling. ❦

THE DING-DING MAN

I WAS RAISED in Kearney, Nebraska, a flat prairie town that felt big only because it was bigger than the neighboring postage stamp communities. We were big enough, at least, to have an ice cream man, who trolled around in a big white panel truck blaring scratchy music through cheap metal loudspeakers attached, barely, to the roof. We would hear him coming, and if we had the energy we'd bother our parents for money and meander over for a sticky ice cream sandwich. There was no mania about it. It was average ice cream, and we were average kids doing our average kid job.

Recently I was in the middle of lacquering a cabinet when I heard the *ding-ding!* of what I now know to be the Ding-Ding Man. That's what they call him here in Omaha. I was halfway down the stairs before I even looked down at my legs and asked, "Where are you going, legs? Why are you running?"

It was just a few years ago I had my first such experience. At the sound of the *ding* I blasted out the front door into the street, elbowing my way past my young daughter Kate who, although she had a considerable head start, also had shorter legs. She did not glare at me with her "I can't believe you just elbowed past your own daughter" look, but stayed focused on the Ding-Ding Man, who I am certain had plenty of ice cream sandwiches for all of us. There was no need to run, or elbow, or tackle.

I go to the grocery store nearly every day. They have fifty times more ice cream choices for half as much money as Mr. Ding-Ding. I don't body-check little old ladies out of the way to get at my Double Butter Fudge Swirl. I almost never get any ice cream at all.

It must be something about that ding-ding.

In 1978, I watched with grim fascination as Jim Jones convinced hundreds of followers to leave beautiful San Francisco to build him a city in the sweaty bushes of Guyana. When some cult members later complained that they wanted to go back home, he commanded them all to drink poisoned grape Flavor-Aid, and nine hundred of them obeyed.

Jones looked a whole lot like Roy Orbison. We all listened happily enough to Orbison singing *Sweet Dreams Baby* or *Pretty Woman,* but if Roy had ever followed a song with, "And now we shall all drink the cyanide-laced lemon-lime!" we would have turned our backs and put on a Beatles album.

I would have thought I was immune to such lemur-like devotion. But ding-ding me and I'll be crossing my yard at a dead run, front door still banging wide open like the lid of a Jack-in-the-box.

Last summer the Ding-Ding Man came down my street ringing his bell in random, weird rhythms. "You're not doing it right," I thought, feeling a little put off at not being properly seduced. It was almost a religious offense. I stayed clear of that guy, that impostor, expecting him to be smitten by the hand of God as he messeth with Thine Holy Ding. He was either smitten or fired, because I never saw him again.

I wish someone could ring a ding-ding bell and compel us all to be kind to each other. I guess it is nice enough that someone can compel me to eat an ice cream sandwich.

After writing this, I called Kate and apologized for knocking her off her stride with my elbow that day. "It's okay, Dad," she said, shrugging it off. "I tried to trip you from behind, but I missed."

That's my girl. ❦

F#CKING SNAKES

IT RAINED HARD FOR DAYS. Set a record, they say. Noah-worthy stuff. The Midwestern drought was over, just like that. When the sun shone down again, all manner of God's creatures crept forth from their shelter. The neighborhood bunnies marched right up to me for some raisin bread, too hungry, ragged and weary for any timid protocol. Their eyes said, "Can we just cut to the chase here, and get something to eat?" A resurrection of ants rose right up through my brick patio, bringing the supporting sand with them. Mosquitoes murmured, circled and organized, plotting to carry off one of my cats.

And — *dammit* — snakes!

Goddammit, I hate snakes. I mean, I like snakes for their beauty and remarkable construction. I even played with them when I was a kid. They make crawling on one's belly look easy. I've tried it, and it is not. But *dammit,* I hate it when they pop out of my garden unexpectedly. Five million years of human evolution kicks in: my adrenaline goes from zero to red-lined in a split-second while I spring up vertically and squeal like a girl. *Dammit!*

Instincts: 1, Pride: 0.

I read recently that a full menu of latent fear instincts is built into all of us, but each instinct needs to be triggered, or it will eventually fade away. For example, you have the wiring to be afraid of snakes, but if, in your individual upbringing, no one flips out over a snake, your jumpy instinct will remain unactivated and you will not experience that fear of snakes. So sometime before my tenth year of life my dad must have been startled by a snake, making him jump and screamed like a girl, and my Yikes reflex was switched on. Thanks, Dad.

On that first sunny day after the rains, I was enjoying lunch outside on my patio. Trying to, anyway, since I couldn't relax while ants were grain by grain dismantling the patio. And of course the patio bricks were sunny, warm and dry, and the garden was dark, chilly and wet. One long green snake could not resist sssssslithering out to the bricks, nearer and nearer to my ticklish bare feet. I tried to relax. Be cool, Mr. Snow White, Mr. Loves-All-Animals-For-What-They-Are. Keep reading your book. Live and let live. But my toes were screaming at my brain: *"Snaaaaake! Sah-nake!"* I flailed my arms a bit and he scurried off. Then [rustle rustle rustle] he crept out again. *Dammit!* I get shivers just writing about it. I waved my arms again. He scurried. He returned again. Repeat.

I gave up and went inside. He probably took over the warm spot in my empty chair. Bastard.

Today the temperature is cooler, so snakes are working harder to get warm. I went up to water the flowers in my butterfly garden, and — *dammit!* — there's a bug-eyed snake that had shinnied up one of the plants, head bobbing and grinning and licking at the breeze as if some flutist had coaxed him out of a basket. (If a flute brings snakes out, is there an instrument to drive them back? Maybe bagpipes?)

Last summer I was happily reading on my little brick front porch, watching joggers jiggle by. I happened to glance down, and there was a snake's head rising out of a crack in the bricks just three inches from me, about to creep into my pocket. My bag of corn chips exploded with a *dammit!* all over the yard, and the neighbor dogs all perked up, seeking the source of that high-pitched squeal.

Do snakes do that on purpose? Do they nudge each other with their scaly little tails and hiss, "Carl, watch thisss guy when I sssneak up on him — it'sss hilariousss!"

Dammit! 🐭

SHED A LITTLE LIGHT

I HAVE A BIG OLD FLASHLIGHT, of a color I call Construction Yellow. It's one of two available tool colors, the other being Construction Orange. I don't know why construction stuff is yellow. If you really want something to stand out in a construction zone, make it pink. A flashlight might as well be any color, since you only use it in the dark.

The flashlight is now the color of spilled paint flecks, amber varnish, that sticky cream-colored aerosol spray expanding foam, and various other 100-year-old-building drippings. I love it for its Jackson Pollock authenticity. It is a scrapbook of the redecorating job I did, restoring an old mortuary into a music venue. Never trust a handyman who has clean tools.

Anyway, when I needed it, my flashlight was dead.

Flashlights are not complicated. There is a battery, a bulb, a wire, a switch. I replaced the batteries. Nothing. I tested the bulb with a couple of wires, and it worked fine. To test the switch itself I reached for my continuity tester, which is basically another flashlight with pointy probes. When I pulled it out from the bottom of my toolbox, where every tool I need always is, one of its wires snagged on the claw of a hammer and snapped.

No problem. I can fix that. As I reassembled the parts, I forgot to put the protective rubber shield back on the pointy prod, so when I put the tool away it dutifully tested the continuity of everything in my toolbox until the battery ran dead.

To replace the battery in the continuity tester you have to remove the teeny light bulb, which is held in place by a teeny little screw. No problem — I have a teeny little screwdriver. Somewhere. Probably at the bottom my toolbox. Couldn't find it. I dumped out the entire toolbox, which is okay because the box was full of sawdust and miscellaneous screws and such, and needed cleaning anyway. Ahhh, there it is! The very last tool at the bottom.

I unscrewed the teeny little screw and, to my great surprise, I didn't drop it. Next I tried to extract the bulb. It crushed like a robin's egg between my fingers. That's okay, the hardware store carries little bulbs like that. In fact, I discovered that the hardware store carries three different little bulbs that look exactly like that, because that's how many trips it took me before I came home with the right one.

The young female clerk who smiled sweetly at me the first time began giving me that "buzz off, stalker" glare by the third trip. Coincidentally, they were having a sale on flashlights, so I bought a new one just in case, so I didn't have to come back again and risk a restraining order.

In an unexpected watershed of fortune, I fixed the bulb in the continuity tester, which I then used to fix the switch in the flashlight. I paused for a moment of self-congratulations as I admired the new pencil-sized flashlight I had bought on sale, all tiny shiny metallic black.

It came with a "carrying case," a little canvas pouch the same size as the flashlight. The case had no loop or hook or anything, so it wasn't so much a carrying case as it was a little flashlight sleeping bag. The flashlight came in plastic packaging big enough to hold a chain saw, and as I threw it away I noticed on the features list that my new flashlight had an "adjustable beam." Really? I was excited to try that feature out, but when I turned it on, the flashlight didn't work. ❦

WHAT GOES AROUND

M Y FRIENDS ARE IN A TIZZY. E-mails firing back and forth. "What is the world coming to? It's just so wrong!"

Nope, not about George Bush. Not Iraq/Afganistan. This fuss was all about Pluto: astronomers had proposed kicking the little planet out of the solar system.

It's as if my parents had said, "We've decided on some new rules, and, well — sorry, but you're not our son anymore." Actually, there were a few times my parents might have tried such a tactic, but I had already made it clear that I knew the state statutes regarding custody. They couldn't dump me off on the state unless I was certifiably crazy, and I was careful to stay just within the boundry.

It's like any party, though: if you let Pluto in, you gotta let everyone in. With our new high-powered telescopes, you'd gain a new planet every two days. We'd run out of names. I can envision sixty planets, including the Verizon "Can You Hear Me *Now?*" planet and the FedEx "We Deliver Anywhere" planet.

But the newly proposed rules have problems too. According to the new scientific definition, my Uncle Boy qualifies a planet.

First, yes — that is his name. When he was born, his parents just referred to him as "Boy," and — it being harvest season — they never really got around to giving him a proper name. Or if they ever did, they didn't bother to tell anyone. To this day, he's Uncle Boy.

So here are the new planet rules, as proposed by the International Astronomical Union:

1. *The object must orbit the sun.* (Uncle Boy does, I suppose, along with the rest of us.)
2. *It must have enough mass to become round.* (Technically, Uncle Boy's mass comes *from* his being round, but the end result is the same.)
3. *It has to have "cleared its neighborhood."* That is definitely Uncle Boy. After his third serving of chili, our last family reunion ended early.

Obviously I am not comfortable with the new rules. I just can't see teaching my kids, "...then comes Mars, and...let's see...there's Jupiter, Uranus, Neptune, and Uncle Boy."

Can't we just keep Pluto? Pluto was admitted before the rules were changed. Couldn't we add some kind of grandfather clause? How about:

4. *Or was already considered a planet prior to August 2006.*

I am as close as I will ever get to having a context in which to contribute the following tidbit: Earth is the only planet on which you can fall down and hurt yourself. All the other planets are either 1) too soft, or; 2) have too little gravity. For example, Mars is made of perfectly hard, sharp rocks, but it has so little gravity that if you tripped and fell, you'd just waft down to the ground like a potato chip. Jupiter's gravity is

2.5 times that of Earth, so that a 200-pound Earth man on Jupiter falls with the weight of a 500-pound oaf. But the ground is as soft as cotton candy, so — *piff* — he doesn't get hurt.

Now that's my kind of planet. 🐭

WEARING MY ART
ON MY SLEEVE

I OWNED A MUSIC VENUE, and touring bands played there all the time. When the Navigators stopped by, they gave me one of their T-shirts. It's a great, one-of-a-kind shirt: soft, olive green with a cool, retro logo. I had it on for about ten minutes before dripping a tomato stain on it.

I slouch backwards when I eat. Tall people do that, because they don't fit well in regular chairs. Our knees stick up. I think that is because most chairs are made by the Chinese, and I'm sure their chairs fit them just fine. I tend to lean back, put my feet up on the chair in front of me, balance my plate over my belly and do crossword puzzles.

Tomatoes and basil are ripe in my garden right now, so almost every day brings bruschetta and wine for dinner. Last week it was a work of art. Not the food — my shirt.

My very first bite dripped juicy red tomato onto my fresh white shirt. There's no wiping that off successfully, any more than one could wipe off a gunshot wound.

It was hard at first, accepting that the shirt was spoiled, not to mention accepting that I was a slob. Before I had even finished feeling embarrassed about myself, *plat!* — a bit of mozzarella slimed with olive oil slid off the edge of the bread onto my chest.

I couldn't help but notice that the first stain bore a striking resemblance to Italy. That seemed appropriate: tomato, basil and mozzarella are innately Italian. Indeed, they make up the colors of the Italian flag. And the mozzarella had landed right where the Vatican would be.

Plop! Yep, that piece of pimiento looks just like the Leaning Tower of Pisa, except it slid off my soft, happy belly and bounced over to where Egypt would be. My hands were dripping with oily tomato and garlic...oh, heck, why not? I just wiped the whole mess on my shirt.

It feels good to commit. It was liberating. I half-expected some props guy to pull up and complete the picture by setting me up with a mobile home and a three-legged pit bull.

Yesterday I wore a bib for the first time since I was a baby. I didn't spill a drop. What's up with that? ❦

MR. IMPORTANT

I MUST BE VERY IMPORTANT.

I suspected it when I planned a vacation. As a bar owner I do a lot of different jobs, and I had to get someone else to cover them. I have college degrees in psychology and philosophy, so I had to find someone equally qualified to take out the trash, pick up cigarette butts, water the plants, and refill the paper towel dispensers.

I do inventory and ordering on Mondays. On Wednesdays I wait around at the bar eating our "Sweet & Spicy" snack mix and drinking tequila until the deliveries show up. I had to train Holli, my bartender, to do that job. She was suspiciously good at eating our snack mix and writing checks.

I discovered upon my return that three out of the four bathroom paper towel dispensers were empty, so it's clear that if my plane had gone down, someone would have eventually missed me. "Remember the good old days when Michael was around?" they'd reminisce. "Those paper towels were a nice touch."

To demonstrate how important I am, the gods made sure that every fascinating event imaginable happened in Omaha the five days I was out of town. I'm a fan of songwriter Gillian Welch, and I was irked to discover she was scheduled to perform in town while I was away. But I left anyway. You can imagine how I felt upon learning that, while she was in town, she stopped into my bar.

With her friend Conor Oberst.

And they played a little impromptu free show.

Indeed, something special happened every single night I was gone. That's how I know I'm Very Important. Why else would the gods bother to mock me so?

Yet I left anyway, leaving the gods shaking their heads. "Man," they said, looking at each other and shrugging, "that dude must have *really* needed a vacation." ❧

I NEED TO PROCESS

IN 1980 I MARRIED into a political family. People I didn't know gave my bride and I many wedding gifts, including three identical toaster ovens and two food processors. When we divorced I was awarded custody of one of each, along with a pillow, a toothbrush, a pencil, and our charge card statement.

I didn't have much space at my new apartment, but I did have a toaster and an oven, so I gave away the toaster oven. But I kept the food processor, because — well, I wasn't exactly sure what a food processor was, and I might need one of those. For...that. For the next twenty years it sat unused in its original box in my basement.

At the first sign of freeze each year I gather all the remaining basil from my garden and grind it up into pesto. I use the traditional, centuries-old method: throw it all in a blender, kind of like a salad daquiri. My garden produces about fifty blenderloads of basil. It takes all evening, but that's okay because I eat pesto and drink wine the whole time. When you are drinking wine and eating Italian food, time isn't much of an issue.

I don't know why, but this year I decided it was time to break out that food processor, and figure out what "processing" food was all about. The 20-year-old manual was a treat in itself. It presumed I must be female. Why else would I have a food processor? The hand-drawn illustrations all looked like Betty Crocker cartoons. The first recipe was for meat loaf. I slipped into my apron.

There is nothing girly about a food processor. The first thing I noticed when I lifted it out of the box was that the drive motor weighed about fifty pounds. This is not an "appliance." It is a power tool. When I turned on the switch, the motor snapped up to speed, making the same confident purr as my radial arm saw. *Buummmmm*. "Dang!" I smiled. I tightened my apron, and grabbed my shop glasses.

The second thing I noticed is that the motor is so powerful it doesn't slow down when you toss things into it. It's like those huge yellow grinders the city uses to eat trees. *Grrooooomp!* My friend and I fed into it the entire summer's worth of basil in about twenty seconds. We hesitated, looking at each other in wide-eyed awe for a few seconds, before searching around for other things to throw in.

"Do you have any carrots?" my friend asked.

"Why? Why would I want ground carrots?"

"Because it'd be cool."

Soon I had a year's supply of diced jalapeños and a ten-lifetime supply of habaneros. (To be fair, a lifetime supply is not that many habaneros, because when you eat them, your life shortens.)

I've written three songs about killing people, although I've never really done it. But if I ever do, I know how I'll dispose of the body.

Grrooooomp!

Right now I'm gazing down upon my withering fall garden — saggy tomato plants, drooping vegetables, wilting flowers. I'm thinking, if I balanced that food processor right over my compost pile...

Grrooooomp! ❦

SEEING SPOTS

I WAS PROBABLY FIVE OR SIX YEARS OLD when *101 Dalmatians* came out. (The first time.) I was bedazzled. According to the box, Life cereal — my favorite, given the choices Mom offered, which were Life cereal or Shredded Wheat — was hosting a sweepstakes: 101 lucky contestants would win a Real Live Dalmatian Puppy!

101 winners?! I didn't even know one other person who ate Life cereal. Mom ate Shredded Wheat. I ran the odds through my head, and clearly I was a shoo-in to win.

Would I get to choose the puppy? I imagined myself half-buried in a pile of pup squeaks, downy fuzz and tiny tongues, trying to select my favorite. Or would they just send me one? I didn't care. I considered the possibility that, if no one else entered, I might get *all* of them. And — this was unprecedented — my mom said it was okay. Her exact, unrevokeable promise: "If you win one, you can keep it." I could scarcely believe she said that, given that all my previous whining for a dog had gotten me no better than a black, bug-eyed goldfish.

I carefully cut off the box top, filled it out and mailed it in. I knew it would take a couple of days for the mail to go back and forth, so I tried to relax for four days before I took my position on the front porch to wait for the mailman.

We didn't get a lot mail back then. Sometimes a letter or a bill or a Sears catalog. Usually, nothing. Certainly a puppy in a box wasn't going to get past me, unnoticed in a pile of junk like I get every day now. I didn't want the poor puppy to be left alone and confused in a dark box on a strange front porch, so every day I sat and waited, perking up at the first sight of the scruffy-haired mailman as he came up the walk, framed between our two massive elm trees.

I have very vivid memories of waiting. The hiss of passing car tires, college students bicycling by on their way to class. I have no memories of giving up, but at some point I must have given up, because here I am in Omaha, Nebraska, with no puppy.

Sometimes you can make things happen by wanting them *that bad*. I've experienced it often in my life, so often that I'm careful about what I wish for. Perhaps it didn't work for the puppy because I was too little at the time. I certainly couldn't have yearned for it harder.

Two years ago, rockabilly guitarist Lash LaRue was inspired to start a toy drive to benefit children of the Pine Ridge Indian Reservation. Among the poorest areas in the United States, it is only a few hours from rich, fat Omaha, my hometown. Those children don't get toys at Christmas, so Lash rustled up a truckload of great stuff: bicycles, games, dolls, musical instruments, and drove it all up there in a donated rental truck. The reservation kids were pie-eyed.

One little boy had his heart set on a ball. He had never owned a ball. The image in my head of Lash, a lanky-limbed, tattooed Santa-in-a-

cowboy-hat, grinding up in a ten-ton rental truck was so...well of *course*
Lash would bring him a ball. How could he not? And indeed Lash did
bring exactly one soccer ball — which some other kid nabbed.

Time stopped.

The little boy froze in statue-like unreality. How can you want
something *that bad,* just *know* you're going to get it, come so close that
you can see it and...have it pass before your eyes and go into someone
else's hands?

Time started again. The child collapsed in heartbreak to the floor
of the swirling, bustling, happy social hall.

Word of the drama found its way to Lash. Having a little Lakota
spirit himself, he began trading, this toy for that, that one for the next
thing. It took about fifteen swaps, but he finally got the ball to the little
boy, who spent the rest of the day attached to Lash's leg.

Sometimes you can make things happen by wanting them *that bad.*
But how could I have wanted a puppy more than I did?

My dad died a few years ago on the 4th of December, after a very
long illness, his lungs slowly stolen by emphysema. At his funeral I was
bolstered to see all his interesting friends — professors, sailors and
radio-controlled airplane pals — gathered in little groups, sharing
stories of my dad. There was more laughter than I expected at a funeral,
but I liked it.

One old man with a dramatic shock of shaggy white hair caught
my eye, but I couldn't quite place him. I could tell that I caught his eye
too. After a long mutual look, the old man hobbled closer to me,
peering deeply, then rose up straight and put his hands on his hips.
"Why, I remember you!" he smiled with satisfaction. "I used to deliver
your mail. You were always sitting there on your front porch..." ❦

THE MEANING OF LIFE

A FRIEND WAS ASKING ME a long list of benign questions. "What time are we supposed to arrive? What should we wear?" Then, noting my annoyance, she added just to be funny, "What is the meaning of life?"

I did what I always do when I don't know the meaning of something. I looked it up. I keep a dictionary in almost every room, because there's a lot I don't know.

For such an ethereal question, the dictionary was full of literal answers. "Life: The period from birth to death." Well, *duh*. Or this: "The quality that distinguishes a functional being from a dead one." *How enlightening!* I can only guess what their definition of "dead" is. "That quality that distinguishes a nonfunctional being from a live one." Sheesh.

But one definition farther down the list aroused my imagination: "The sequence of physical and mental experiences that make up the existence of an individual." According to that, your life isn't just what you do — it's also what you *think* about what you're doing. Or even just what you think about. My daydreams are thus as much a part of my life as bumping my head.

I plan on living pretty much forever. My dad smoked continuously. Each fresh cigarette he lit had to nudge out the butt of the previous one. He drank beer and buttermilk with every meal, and still blew past 70 years old. My mom has beautiful, thick, salt-and-pepper hair and great teeth, and the skin on her face glows like pearls, so pretty that you want to touch it. So genetically, I'm set.

Now Harvard has just published this bombshell: wine really does make your life healthier. And boy, have I been taking my medicine.

Rats, put on a high-blubber diet and given huge doses of wine extract, performed just as well on agility and exercise equipment as rats given nothing but proper food and exercise and who, accordingly, wanted to shoot themselves. Indeed, the healthy-life rats, when given the opportunity, ran on treadwheels and pressed levers feverishly in an attempt to get into the other group.

This has not been tested yet on humans, but I imagine there will be quite a queue of volunteers for the study. The rats got a dosage that was the human equivalent of one hundred bottles of red wine a day. Fortunately, I owned a bar and could buy wholesale.

I trust that the meaning of life goes beyond drinking a hundred bottles of wine. But as fad diets go, it sure beats bulking up on fiber and fresh vegetables. ❦

I'M ATTACHED

I COULDN'T BELIEVE MY EARS. A woman told me I have a problem with attachments. She said it's probably because I'm a Pisces.

I know a lot about astrology. I've been told I drink too much and dream too much and reinterpret reality too much and guess at what you're thinking too much and trust Heaven too much because I'm a Pisces. But when it comes to attachments, Pisces or not, I don't think I have any problems at all.

Right now, without leaving my chair, I can reach a screwdriver that has eight assorted replaceable heads. I have a fat orange battery-powered screwdriver (well, sort of orange — it's covered in all manner of paint splatters and glue drips) and it has a drill attachment which snaps right over the screwdriver head. It's hardly even an attachment, really. More of a little hat. Drill, screw, drill, screw — no waiting.

When its battery finally gave out, I could have replaced it with some young new thing. But you don't just throw away something you're attached to like that. You work on it, nurture it, fix it and move on. The dings and stains become beautiful to you over time. They are the memories and milestones of the relationship you had. They are what made it mine.

It's women who don't care for attachments. I gave both of my daughters a Leatherman — that pliers-meets-Swiss Army knife tool that explodes into a bouquet of micro-tools, all too small to be of any real use, but still comforting to look at. Sure, they use it, and they're grateful for it. But they don't get it out and pet it, dreaming of saving someone's life by having just the right tiny Phillips in the nick of time. And I'm sure they don't call it a Leatherman, because they don't know a Leatherman from a Stanley from a Craftsman. I bet they call it That Tool Thingy Dad Gave Me.

A Swiss Army knife is barely even a tool, but more an artwork of pure attachment, the only usable item being the corkscrew, which nobody ever uses because Swiss Army knives and wine are never found on the same person. But guys will see that corkscrew and think, "Well, good to have one just in case."

At one point the company tried to appeal to women by making the knives pink, as if the only reason women weren't flocking to get a Swiss Army Knife was because they didn't look good in red. That's what I bought my daughters: pink Swiss Army knives, so small they didn't even have corkscrews. I don't know what I was thinking.

I just bought a wireless earpiece for my cell phone. Now, is that an attachment, or not? ❧

X MARKS THE SPOT

My FRIEND JEFF just got back from Dallas. He toured the site of John Kennedy's assassination, and was impressed with how touristy the place was. I'm surprised too. In my Benson neighborhood, when we shoot someone, we hush it up. We don't put up a gift shop.

I learned through a marketing class that customers prefer to shop where there are the fewest gunshots. So I was surprised to learn that in Dallas, they've marked a big red X on the street where Kennedy was shot, so you can go stand in traffic and have your picture taken by your mom from up in the Book Depository window. For a fee, you can go up to the Depository warehouse window and imagine yourself as Lee Harvey Oswald. Actually, what they take you to is the window next to Lee's. They won't let you look out the real window.

The museum offers a live web cam view from the real Book Depository window. You can log on at any time, from anywhere, and see if there's anyone, right now, you might like to shoot.

When you are finished pretending you have shot JFK, you are herded to the museum gift shop. It is fat with souvenirs like the Grassy Knoll Shot Glass and the JFK Action Figure with Replaceable Head.

Jeff and I pondered "grassy knoll." When you refer to the grassy knoll, you never have to specify *which* grassy knoll you mean, even though every knoll is grassy. The thing is, nobody ever uses just the word *knoll.* Granted, I've always lived in Nebraska, where if you claim to be polysyllabic they think you're a Mormon and invite you to attend a "real" church. But still, it's not a knoll, it's a *hill.* I looked up *knoll* and the word is rooted, pardon the pun, in the German word for tuber. Tubers are never grassy. I suspect that when a cop said, "The shot came from that grassy hill!" some novelist, making ends meet by moonlighting as a cub reporter, grabbed his Thesaurus. *"Hill?* No, that's too boring. Lessee, *drumlin*...no...*mound*...nah...*butte, hummock, slope*...oh, here we go — *knoll!"*

I checked: entire websites are devoted to people arguing over who first used the term "grassy knoll," so I'm not the only one who thinks about it. I suppose it's better than saying "grassy hill," and then always having to say which grassy hill you mean.

We don't have any tourist attractions in my Benson neighborhood. Our "Shot-Dead Robber of the Week!" website didn't generate many visitors. Presidents don't ever come parading down Maple Street, and even if one did and you took a shot at him from the second floor window of the From Here to Maternity Bra Shop, you might miss and accidentally hit Saddle Creek Records and kill Conor Oberst, and then his labelmates would all write a song about it and make a million dollars.

I'm already sorry I put that idea in their heads. Right now Conor is backing away from the front window while his fellow musicians are picking at their soul patches, thinking, "Hmmmm..." ❦

GO AWAY

A COUPLE OF YEARS AGO when I added another phone line, my cable company, Cox, gave me free HBO. I didn't really care about HBO, but it was free, so thanks.

A year later, sufficiently happy with my new cell phone, I canceled the cable land line. Like a jealous boyfriend, Cox snatched back that free HBO. But fine, fair, okay, whatever — there are only so many times a guy can watch *Titanic* anyway, waiting for that one good nude scene, and the part where Jack — *finally* — drowns.

Then before she hung up, the customer service woman I had called added, "And there will be a $17 charge to disconnect the HBO."

"Ho! Wait a minute," I replied. "You can't charge me to not have something. I don't pay to have things taken away from me."

That wasn't really true. I once gave a neighbor kid $5 to go away.

The woman's graceful, helpful demeanor immediately morphed into Sista Stompin Ballgrindaz, which I took as evidence that she faced this battle every day. So I gave her a break and asked for her supervisor, who was nice at first too.

"Well, you see," the supervisor explained as if I were six years old, "it's because they have to climb the pole to disconnect the HBO."

"I see." I didn't see. "So just skip climbing the pole. Save yourself seventeen bucks."

I omit the ensuing give-and-take except to say I enjoyed for once being on the strong side of an argument. She eventually canceled the charge. After all, what was she going to do if I didn't pay it? Cancel my cancellation?

We were all settled and satisfied, insidiously polite, saying goodbye when she dropped the bomb: "Thank you for choosing Cox!"

Oh, *dammit*. We were *soooooo close*. Why did she have to go say something like that?

"I'm *not* choosing Cox," I clarified. "I'm specifically *not* choosing Cox. I nearly paid $17 to *not choose Cox*."

When the foot-dragging, saggy-eyed technician showed up exhausted at 7pm on that cold, windy winter evening (apparently lots of people canceled HBO that day), it took all I had to refrain from saying, "Dude, here's seventeen bucks. Skip the pole and go on home." That would have been worth it, endless *Titanic* reruns or not. ❦

BETTER OILY THAN LATE

MARIA CASTILLO DIED OF A SHOT TO HER BUTT. It wasn't a gunshot, but a lethal injection of "beauty oil."

Earlier, beautician Martha Vasquez had convinced Maria that a $1,400 shot of her secret "French polymer" would smooth out Maria's cellulite. Besides being a killer, Martha was a big fat liar because her oil wasn't a polymer. It wasn't even French. It was Mazola corn oil.

Martha claimed it was an "anti-aging treatment." I guess she got that part right, since Maria is no longer aging.

Which is worse: a wrinkly butt or an oily one? If the goal is to reduce wrinkles, I would suggest an injection of an air compressor hose. You never see a wrinkly blimp.

Botox was invented to smooth wrinkles by immobilizing your face altogether. It leaves one with that blank, emotionless expression I'm so used to seeing on people when I tell stories. Too big a dose and your face melts down to your chest, a slurring slobbering mess as if you just came from the dentist. So maybe corn oil was worth a try, in hopes that everything would just slide flat.

If you injected your face full of oil, would there be a risk that your eyes and mouth would slip and slide into all sorts of unintended expressions? *Whoops!* You try to smile and all of a sudden your lips meet on the back of your head.

One of the things I like about European films is that the actors almost never wear make-up. They look like people, which makes them more believable since that's what they're trying to act like. Bob Barker is trying to imitate a game show host, but his spackled-on smile gives me the creeps. I know he pries it off and hangs it on a hook at the end of the day, just like Michael Myers.

(This has nothing to do with anything, but I don't think I'll ever again get this close to having a context in which to share this tidbit: In *Halloween,* the original Michael Myers mask, terrifying in its Botox-blandness, was a repainted William Shatner mask the props crew got at a costume shop. And now, back to our story.)

If there is anything to be learned, it is this: if you are shy about your wrinkly butt, just turn the lights down. Or put pants on. Don't do anything that'll kill you.

In other words, don't be too oily, and don't be late. ❦

I SWEAR

I GOT HOME LATE. I was exhausted. I headed straight to bed. Just as I dozed off, at that dreamy point when all thoughts and sounds echo lightly in the brain, I faintly heard that tell-tale *fht-fht-fht-fht-fht.*

My subconscious mind radioed my literal brain like a World War II movie's submarine alarm. *Aawooo! Aawooo!*

Bat!

I tried to focus in the dark. Sure enough, there he was, chasing my ceiling fan, circling all flappy like a bad movie prop on a string. Out the bedroom door he went. A moment of quiet. Then back in, twice around the ceiling fan, then back out the door. He had the whole house to terrorize.

Clever me, I opened the bedroom window to let him out the next time he flapped in. The bat didn't fly out, but my two cats did, leaping like reindeer into the night. Luckily (depending on how you feel about cats) they landed on my porch roof. I called to them in a scream-whisper, trying not to wake my neighbors. They were too scared to move, and I was too scared to climb out onto the steeply angled roof.

Spek, my favorite of the two cats, began inching along the gutter, farther and farther away. An emergency rescue was on. Cue the ominous kettle drums.

It was now three o'clock in the morning as I, uniformed in my saggy-butt boxer shorts, drug my rickety wooden ladder to the front yard. I knew I had about five minutes before someone called the police to report a man in his underpants trying to crawl into an open window.

When you try to snatch a scared cat off a roof while you're standing on a high ladder, your second thought is, "I should have worn more protective clothing." Or clothing, at least. Your first thought is unprintable.

I returned to bed, heart pounding, adrenaline pulsing, and tic-tac-toed with red, welting scratches. Then I remembered I still had a bat. Now tired *and* mad, I shut my window, slammed my bedroom door closed, and promised to evict the bat in the morning. What I didn't realize was that, at that moment, the bat was in the bedroom with me when I shut the door.

A bat makes a certain noise when it lands on your head. When a bat lands on my head, I make a certain noise too.

The bat barely missed me on each lap around the bedroom while I crawled on my hands and knees to open the window again, after a quick scan for cats. Then I went down to the basement to get leather gloves (see? I learned about protective clothing!) and while I was down there I felt something with my bare toes.

I don't know why there was a snake in my basement, and I don't know how I learned to fly.

This time I did not make a noise — at least not within the audible range of human hearing — even though my lungs emptied as if I'd wrung out a rag.

The next morning began with a wasp landing on the back of my hand. I got up, walked it out the back door, and it flew off. "Good karma," I thought. Then a spider as big as a quarter dropped from the ceiling while I was in the shower. I felt like the Snow White of vermin.

Afterwards, I calmed myself with a nice warm cappuccino, carrying it to my cozy, sunny office. As I sat down in my chair, the bat popped out of my wastebasket. *Yowlp!* I blew the next half-hour cleaning cappuccino from the ceiling.

I think bats are fascinating — beautiful, even — when I know I'm coming up on one or they're in a glass box. But when they just pop out at me, all squeaks and clicks and spazz and flippity-floppity, I drop to the ground and release every swear word I know in one long, hyphenated string. Nothing adds vim and vigor to a swear word like being scared, mad, and embarrassed all at the same time.

Bats drop by every August. Experts say it's a migration thing. Young bats don't have a good handle on where they are supposed go, and sometimes they get lost. That makes me feel more sympathetic, because I know how teenagers can be. But I swear, even though I know they're coming *sometime,* I still squeal like a girl. I hate that. This bat came out of my wastebasket. Last year it was one coming up the basement stairs as I was going down. The year before that I was dive-bombed in my kitchen. And the Granddaddy Swear-Word-Generator-of-All-Time was when I was checking insulation in the cramped crawlspace of my attic and one dropped from the insulation into my lap, attached itself to my inner thigh, then fell back asleep. I couldn't even swear out loud, for fear of waking it. My jaw nearly cracked as I clamped it shut. I had to *oooch* down the stairs and out the front door, walking on my butt cheeks before attempting to flick him into the yard. Once free of him, my swear words came out in alphabetical order.

Europeans are the best swearers. When Americans curse, it's mostly a disjointed listing of activities centered primarily between the navel and the knee. Europeans, they create scenarios. A single swear event might have a cast of characters ranging from Mother Mary to familiar barnyard animals. Maybe it's because they have more bats in Europe.

Here's a little tip: if you think there is a bat in your house but you can't find him, he's probably in your curtains. Trust me on that one. ❦

GERM WELFARE

IF YOU HAVE LICE and you plink one out of your hair, you are holding a louse. If something is like a louse, it's lousy. It's kind of like the word measly, which we use to mean "meager," but which literally means "covered in measles."

Now that we have come to terms, why do measly, lousy vermin hitch a ride on humans in the first place? I've never seen a cat with the measles. And for all their catting around, cats never get gonorrhea. (I am proud to say I spelled that correctly after only three tries.)

Germs have as much a right to exist as any of us, but why don't they inhabit something safer, something that doesn't fight back so vehemently as humans do? Why not infect a potato?

Potatoes don't complain about anything. They don't cry out even when you rip them from their warm earth home and plop them into boiling oil with salt and pepper. Maybe they cry on the inside, but a lousy, measly, gonorrheal spud will just endure its fate. I think potatoes are the most stoic of vegetables. Potatoes exist without emotion. Potatoes are British.

So why do germs infect humans and not potatoes? Germs just want to have fun, travel, and see the world. Potatoes don't.

If a germ were to hitch a ride on a potato, he'd sit in the same dirt for three months, then get plucked out and tossed in hot oil. An uneventful life, not counting that last minute.

Now consider the itinerary of the Good Ship Humanity. A germ hops on me. I pick my nose, pass the germ on to the liquor delivery guy when I return his pen after signing off on the shipment. Our germ then gets a transfer to the shipping manager, who hands it off with a handshake to the sales rep, whom Germ uses to get to the tequila representative, who just announced he's on his way back home to Guadalajara. Once in Mexico, Mr. Germ introduces himself to the mailman, and, although it took six layovers, Mr. Germ is now on vacation, via special delivery to the Pacific beaches of Mexico. *¡Gracias, humanos!* No small potatoes.

This explains why everyone gets sick on a plane. This is why you never get sick before your vacation, but always during it. This is why nobody gets sick traveling to Alaska, and everybody falls ill on the way to Cancún. The reason work-at-home people don't get sick isn't because they're isolated. It's because they don't do anything germs want to do.

This also explains why you get a cold in the winter. That's when you are more likely to book a trip south. In the summer, the best a germ can hope for is a ride on your sweaty back as you mow the yard.

I suppose a germ's desire to vacation someplace warm and humid would also help to explain the transference of STDs. Crotches: the Caribbean of the viral. ❦

TOSSED SALAD

I WATCHED A TV SPECIAL on the rise of Bing Crosby's career. He sharpened his young talents on the vaudeville circuit, which back then was as supportive and nurturing as *The Gong Show.*

Don't remember *The Gong Show?* It was a very funny variety show where three talentless has-beens listened to about a minute of your act, and decided whether to interrupt you by whacking a giant gong with a giant mallet, which meant you were a loser. A gong is a 15th- century Malay instrument originally designed to tell foreign travelers, "You suck. Go home."

One problem with *The Gong Show* was that it was too tempting to whack a gong. Stand in front of one, grab a fat mallet, and — wow, you can't stop yourself, can you? You have this singer or juggler or mime or whatever, singing/juggling/miming his heart out, hoping for his big break, to finally show his family he's not a complete failure, while three attention hogs stand there with a mallet in their twitchy grip. And the camera immediately pans to whoever hit the gong. It wasn't a fair fight.

When they show old vaudeville clips, unhappy audiences can be seen expressing their displeasure by throwing cabbages and tomatoes. I suppose this is because TV wasn't invented yet, so they didn't know they were supposed to bang a gong. Back then, a giant hook on a long stick would creep out from the wings and yank a failing performer off the stage by his neck. This is why Bing could sing and dance so well.

Vaudeville audiences must have had the same itchy problem as the *Gong Show* judges. They brought that tomato all the way from home, obviously half-expecting the show to suck. Why else would they bring a tomato? They were lucky to have made it to the theater without squishing the tomato in their pockets, and they definitely didn't want to bring it back home. So they hold their tomato and watch the show, thinking, "Does he suck enough yet? I need to get rid of this thing."

Indeed, I bet the biggest compliment a performer could hope for was to see a bunch of people on the street after the show, eating their tomatoes.

Don't even start on "Why would they bring a tomato in the first place?" You know why. Imagine being told, "Hey, bring a tomato to the show tonight. If the show sucks, you get to throw it!"

"Seriously?" I'd reply. "Promise?" And I'd be off to the store to buy three, just in case, because I have crummy aim.

I would never bring cabbage, though, because it's awkward and unsatisfying to throw. No splat. Just a *piff.*

Times have changed. These days people don't bring tomatoes to the theater because tomatoes are now bred to travel, tough and dry and hardskinned. They don't splat like in the good old days. And maybe this is why there's so much junk on television. 🍅

GETTING FRESH

HERE'S A THOUGHT-PROVOKING FAD DIET: only eat what's fresh within one hundred miles of your house. This diet isn't so much about being skinny as it is about being supportive of your neighbors.

In Nebraska, it means eating ham, roast beef, turkey, potatoes, yams, fresh bread and apple pie. Every meal is Thanksgiving dinner.

So this diet is definitely not about being skinny. It was this same diet that nearly emptied Ireland, because there was no good food within a hundred miles. It would have emptied England too, except the English don't seem to care whether food is any good.

Thanksgiving dinner every day isn't a good idea even for one whole day, judging by the supplications to God I hear at the end of every holiday meal. "Oh God, oh Jesus, don't let me explode..."

My problem would be with coffee. I love it. I want it. It's good for me. It doesn't grow within a thousand miles, much less a hundred, of my house. I would have to move to Columbia (nope) or Hawaii (yes!). But in Hawaii the other local food options are pineapples, coconuts and sugarcane (that is, piña coladas) and chocolate-covered macadamia nuts.

This is why Hawaiians are heavily recruited as football linemen, if you can wake them up, and why I would soon be eligible for a job on the end of a string at the Macy's parade.

Californians grow avocados, lemons, limes and every other healthy fruit and fresh vegetable imaginable. This is why they are all skinny, and secretly miserable. This is why all self-help fads start in California: they know they live in paradise, they know they should be happy, but they look at their plate and they cry inside. These culinary evangelicals try to convince the world to eat healthy like they do, because there is comfort in numbers. They are skinny not because they are healthy but because who wants one more lemon? This is why they drink so much wine. They'd drink scotch but it doesn't grow within a hundred miles of them and they can't bear to be unhip.

Midwesterners are fat and happy. In Nebraska, when kids come home crying, teased by rotten, ruthless little friends, the mom is likely to say, "Aw, honey, it's not the end of the world. I just made some chocolate chip cookies. Let's have some ice cream with them and you'll forget all about it." Have a bad day in Los Angeles, and your stepmom will toss you a carrot and a book entitled *Making Friends For Dummies* as she drives off for another Botox shot so her forehead doesn't furrow.

All in all, I'm in good shape as far as local food goes. There's a Kellogg's factory just three miles away. The entire neighborhood smells like Fritos. The asparagus I planted a few years ago is starting to sprout. I got three stalks this spring — about two more than I need. ❦

SUCH A DOLL

A FRIEND OF MINE WAS WORRYING ALOUD because her young son wanted to play with dolls. As for her, she didn't care one bit. But her friends howled their disapproval. She didn't elaborate about her son's desires, but I imagined the boy wanted to do nothing more than arrange the dolls in a circle, and have some nice conversation over tea.

I played with dolls a lot when I was little. Army Men, G.I. Joe. They call them "action figures," but if anyone had an figure meant for action, it was Barbie. Indeed, Barbie and Ken were my first sex education teachers, although they mislead me on a few details.

With my dolls I would plan patiently, meticulously for Imminent Destruction. I'd arrange one team of little army men on this side of the sandbox and opposing little army men over on that side, all poised to fight each other. Even my cat got into the act, burying toxic WMD across the battlefield.

But it was inevitably a Catastrophic Act of God that destroyed both, in the form of my Crashing Foot of Death, or Tornadic Earthquake Hands.

My dad was meticulous about teaching me to use his tools properly. My play armory included a high-speed drill with an auger bit. A plastic hostage might be taken to the basement to face the Tell-Us-What-You-Know Radial Arm Saw, which was in this instance a De-Arm Saw. And nothing instills fear in the little plastic hearts of army men like the *pahh!* sound a propane torch makes when you light it.

As a god, I didn't like people much.

When I was little, video games set you up as the prey. Asteroids, Pac Man, Frogger, Space Invaders — in each game you scrambled piteously for your life, and you inevitably lost it. But now the tables are turned. In today's games, your point of view is aiming down the barrel of your gun. In Frogger, you are no longer run over by the car — you're driving it.

Whenever there is a heinous crime and people mutter, "How could someone *do* something like that?", I can't help but think Mr. Someone has been training his whole life to do something like that. He's been shooting, punching, bombing and torching nameless strangers in video games since he was old enough to quit sucking his thumb, then getting away in a stolen car through city streets at 90mph, and the random squished pedestrian does not even lower his score. His parents paid hundreds for this education, just to keep him out of their hair.

But for the love of God, whatever you do, don't let your son have dolls for a tea party. That could be dangerous. ❦

LEND ME A HAND

MY NEIGHBOR MATT IS GETTING FAMOUS. He makes big bronze sculptures in his studio next door to me. I go over there all the time to see what he's up to and to avoid doing my own work.

A while ago he asked me if I would model for one of his statues. I immediately imagined myself as a naked, sculpted Michelangelo's David, all rippling muscles and buggy-out veins and big hands and — well, you know, big hands.

"Put this on." Matt handed me a baggy lime-green leisure suit. It was a lot like the one I wore to my high school prom, except the prom one fit me. Matt was making a sculpture of a New Orleans jazz musician. "We need to photograph how the pants and jacket drape, so we can get the folds right." After putting on the jacket, I was asked to strike the pose of a wailing trumpet player. This is not the macho gig I hoped for, but I did at least feel qualified, if I may toot my own horn, because I used to watch my dad play the cornet. I played air horn with authority.

I discovered that it is very hard to blare one's horn up to the sky, holding the mute in an outstretched arm, back severely arched, for twenty minutes.

"What in the world did you do to get so hinked up?" my chiropractor asked the next day. I started to explain, but gave up and lied something about a softball game.

A few weeks later Matt called me again. They were having trouble getting the trumpeter's hand to look right. Could I come over again? I was secretly thrilled. I struck my best trumpet hand pose, fingers artistically expressing each heartbreaking note, and he plunged my hand into a tub of liquified latex, which would be used to create a plaster cast. Exciting! Now part of the actual me was going to be in the statue! It was my first hand job.

Months later the statue was finished. It's in front of the Omaha Qwest Center, along with a bunch of other giant bronzes: jugglers, dancers and clowns, 42 pieces in all. I was surprised to discover that the statue I had been posing for was an old black man. I am Scottish. This made it a little harder to convince my friends it was really me up there glistening in bronze.

At least he is on a pedestal — someplace I have always thought I belonged. And I like my new claim to fame. I literally lent him a hand. Every time I pass him I strike the pose.

So the statue's dirty secret is this: although he is an artistic, old black New Orleans jazz musician, a lanky Scottish guy in Omaha is his right hand man. ❦

BONE PHONE

I DON'T LIKE BEING A CROTCHETY OLD LUDDITE reminiscing about the Good Old Days, but when it comes to phones, we are going backward. The last time I had a great phone connection was in 1973.

It was called a bone phone due to the shape of the receiver. The bone phone was a breakthrough in design: the earpiece faced your ear, and the mouthpiece faced your mouth. Genius! In between those ends was a handle that fit comfortably in your hand, or you could wedge it onto your shoulder and hold it with your head. Some phones even came with a little shoulder pillow, making hands-free talking comfortable enough that you could fall asleep listening to your girlfriend. It didn't have batteries so it never went dead. You could talk for hours, unless you had my mom. The always-black bakelite plastic was hard enough that in a pinch you could use it as a hammer.

The first sign of trouble was the introduction of the Princess Phone. It looked modern with its rounded edges — kind of like a sagging brick of taffy — but it was elusive and slippery to hold. I dropped one and it broke, and back then I felt I could fix a broken phone. I pried it open and was surprised to discover it was nearly empty but for some tiny electronics and a lead weight screwed to the body, which the manufacturer added so the phone would feel substantial, and so you wouldn't know it was a frail piece of junk.

Cell phones changed everything, and I'm not going to complain here about how. And I'm not a Luddite — I've used cell phones since we first learned to pronounce Nokia.

I bought my first cell phone so that I could pre-order fast food on the way home from the bar. In fierce Midwestern traffic, that can save you as much as two minutes.

My first cell phone was about the size of a circus hot dog. It had a tiny little screen with pixelly green letters just like early computers. It came with a fat leather case and had an antenna that pulled out like a walkie-talkie. I felt like a secret agent, and learned that I was easier to understand if I talked like Maxwell Smart.

That phone met its end when it was run over by a hearse, which I thought was overkill. Amazingly, the phone still worked, but the screen only displayed oily-black, lava-lamp pop-art puddles. Although they looked cool, I couldn't see what I was dialing, and I had been taught not to speak to strangers.

I went through an evolution of simple phones and fancy phones, phones that flipped open like a clamshell and others that sprung out like a switchblade. What they all had in common was that none offered a clear conversation.

My phone *du jour* has lots of clever ringtones, none of which I can hear. I've learned that if I set it to vibrate and put it in my pocket, I can feel it buzz on my thigh. That works better, and it feels good. When I'm lonely, I call myself.

Lately my thigh has been buzzing even when I don't have my phone. It's disconcerting because there is nothing to answer. I have developed a phantom ring.

It started when I crashed my sailboat twice in one day. My little catamaran is fast but volatile, more or less two big water skis with a trampoline stretched between them to sit on. Lots of sail but not much boat, so it blows over sometimes, and you get bucked off. If your body flies above all the rigging, it's like being thrown by your friends into a cool lake. It's fun. If instead you go *through* all the rigging, it's more like being thrown by your friends into a pinball game.

After doing the latter last weekend, my brain rewired and my left thigh has been randomly buzzing ever since. I go to answer it but the phone is not ringing. Sometimes the phone isn't even there. I tried yelling at my leg: "Who is it?!" but no one was home. An hour later it would ring again. It's like when war veterans lose a limb, and it still itches. Do phantom limbs get phantom phone calls? If you were run over crossing a busy street because you were wearing your earbuds and didn't hear the panicked car horn, and your ears got ripped off, would you still hear your phantom iPod?

My current phone is a tiny, black, slippery rectangle with rounded corners. I drop it just looking at it. There isn't really an ear "piece," just a pinhole big enough to let only little words out. When the ear pinhole is positioned right over my eardrum, the mouth pinhole lines up with my second molar. The reception is such that it works most everywhere except in my home or at my work. This is probably why people talk while they drive: it's the only time they get a decent signal.

I was at the grocery store yesterday when my shorts started to slide down. They are supposed to be held up with a drawstring, but I have no butt for the string to hang on to, and with a growing belly, the string has more than gravity to fight. Normally guys with my problem just stuff their hands into their pockets, then do The Shrug: you grip your pants from inside the pockets and act like you don't care about something, and when you shrug you hike your pants back up, being careful not to grab your underpants too, because you can't gracefully pick them out while at the grocery store.

But I was on the phone so I couldn't shrug. I tried to wedge the slippery phone between my head and shoulder like my old bone phone, to free up both hands for that emergency shrug, but I might as well have been talking on a watermelon seed. The phone kept squirting this way and that.

I was desperately nearing the point of depantsedness, where my beltline passes the equator of my butt and my shorts freefall to my ankles. Squirming and contorting to ooch them back up with one hand, I looked like Joe Cocker.

This would not have happened with the old bone phone. And maybe this explains why, for the last five years, every teenage boy I see has his pants half-assed. "Dude, hang up and shrug!"

"Where are the genius inventors when we need them?" I complained to my friend Marco. "Why don't they make an ergonomic phone, one that doesn't drop calls, one on which I can understand people? We need a Space Age phone!"

"The Space Age," he reminded me, "was 1965." ❦

MAN IN TIGHTS

THE AWKWARD HALLOWEEN COUNTDOWN: every year I have great ambitions of creating some amazing costume, cool and clever, smart and wry. Every year, with Halloween just days away, I still have no clue what my costume will be, and so I head to the novelty store to buy some dumb plastic thing.

I've already been to the costume shop. The choices were endless. My first thought was, we should dress like this every day! Why don't we wear this stuff to work? I'd much rather have a closet full of costumes than one full of drab suits. (Okay, I only own one suit and it no longer fits.) Imagine how much fun it would be to go to work dressed as Bo Peep, anticipating who might be in the next cubicle. A killer bee? Spiderman? Or some randomly weird pun costume that no one gets? It'd be like having new co-workers every day.

Clever pun costumes never work for me. A few years ago I splattered my clothes with paint and stuck on a name tag that said "Hello — my name is Jerzy Kostrzewski." I pranced proudly around the party waiting for someone to point and laugh. "What are you?" they would ask, dully.

"Jackson Polack."

[Long pause.]

"The famous artist." [pause.] "He splattered paint." [Pause.] "Polack/Pollock."

[Pause.]

"Oh," they'd say flatly before heading back to the cheese dip.

[sigh.]

I set a new record last Halloween. A few years ago, wearing a fright wig and fangs custom-made by my dentist friend who otherwise makes regular teeth for a living, I scared three little trick-or-treaters enough to send them scurrying like skidding bunnies into the bellies of their parents. I just stand there — I don't do anything frightening like yell or lunge or offer to sell them magazine subscriptions.

This year's score: five kids ran from my peeling green skin. One parent gave me a first-rate dirty what-kind-of-creep-are-you glare. Lighten up, mom! You just dressed your four-year-old daughter in a skimpy princess dress and sent her alone to the door of a candy-dangling stranger. Who's the scary one here?

My favorite visitor last year was little Jack, whose mom kept repeating, "It's only Michael. He's not really scary."

"I'm not scared," Jack replied, feet planted firmly a safe twenty feet from my front door. "I just have enough candy."

At about 8:30pm, the junior high kids who were too cool and too old to dress up begin arriving, having changed their minds after watching all the little kids rake in the loot. They are always football players or hobos. They thrust open a pillowcase. I save the crappiest candy for them.

My friend Laurie discovered last year that no one would talk to her when she dressed ghoulish. She was really disappointed. But it is weird trying to have a normal conversation with someone who's drooling and bleeding from the eyes. When she was a Sexy Little Devil the year before, in black fishnets and skimpy red sequined dress, everyone wanted to talk to her. I don't know what she's going as this year, but I'll bet she's not going to waste a lot of money on fake blood or clothing.

Just for a change last year I dressed up as a winged fairy. I discovered there is no costume more comfortable than white slippers, pink tights and a tutu. It only scared the adults.

The older I get, the less makeup I need to look scary. This year it only took twenty minutes to look like the walking un-dead.

Next year I'm going to carry around a karaoke machine. What could be scarier than that? ❦

PANNED

I WAS LUCKY ENOUGH TO SCORE an invitation to a Thanksgiving potluck dinner at my friend's house. Laurie's parties are the best: she tarts everything up on a grand scale. I wasn't surprised to encounter three kinds of stuffing, one made with lavender blossoms, another with brandied cherries. She never offers marshmallow and banana Jello, or green bean casserole made with cream of mushroom soup and those crunchy fake onion rings on top, even though she knows full well it's Thanksgiving.

I contributed a cherry chocolate pie with a honey graham cracker crust, and some heart-stopping yams. Not "heart-stopping good," but heart-stopping face to face with St. Peter.

It was a feast fit for gluttons, and we all were stuffed before we even touched the pie I brought, so I just left it. The next day I thought, "Dang, I *really* want a taste of that chocolate pie." So I called Laurie and asked her to save me a slice. Graceless, I know, but if you ever had that pie, you wouldn't have any manners either. She replied flatly, "You can make another pie."

Well, never mind that she has my pie *pan*. I remember I have another pan, not as good as the glass one at her house, but good enough, so fine, I'll make another pie. Except guess where the other pie pan is? At her house, from last year.

Suddenly the sky opened and it all becomes clear. When I had asked her what I could contribute to the meal, she said, "Perhaps a pie." I remember that when I presented the pie to her she said, "I used to have a pan like that..." And the look on her face continued, "...and now I do again."

Now I believe that the trick to holidays is to look around your kitchen to see what things you might need, then throw a party. When guests say, "Can I bring anything?" you can answer, "Why, yes, that would be lovely of you! Perhaps something you can make in a big mixer. You know, one of those nice KitchenAid mixers with the power take-off on the front. A red one."

At my last party someone left behind a huge plastic bowl with a cracked brown lid that was supposed to look like a chocolate chip cookie, but more resembled that novelty store fake vomit which doesn't look like real vomit but doesn't look like a cookie either. It hit me: these guests weren't thinking, "Let's take cookies to the party — now what shall we put them in?" They schemed, "Let's bring cookies, so we can get rid of this ugly-ass bowl."

I am already planning ahead for my annual New Year's Eve party. Would you like to come? We're going to cook up a raft of appetizers, and if you want to contribute something, that'd be fantastic. Something in a nice 9x12 casserole dish, perhaps. Not the cheap metal kind, but one of those nice Pyrex ones... ❦

AMERICAN PARENT

WHEN MY CHILDREN WERE LITTLE, Cabbage Patch dolls were the rage. Really, rage. Before I could even say "I can't believe some idiot would pay $40 for a fat little kid," my wife came home with a black eye she earned fighting over Just The Right Doll at the department store. "You should have seen the other mom," she lisped proudly through a loose tooth.

My kids played respectfully with their Cabbage Patch dolls for about two days, then asked for a My Little Pony. I confess I once bought them a Rainbow Brite sleeping bag — but, hey, they *needed* a sleeping bag.

This year, American Girl dolls are going for $100 a head. The more expensive American Girls come with their own story, so you can save your kids the inconvenience of having to use their imagination.

I just read in the newspaper that parents are flying their children to Chicago to visit American Girl Place, where for about $1200 (airfare included) you can have tea with your doll (not included) and get her hair styled. They actually seat-belt the doll into a stylist's chair. (I suppose at

$100 a pop, you don't let your doll fall out of her seat.) Moms are crowing about the quality time they are having with their daughters. Quality time with my parents never involved airfare.

For half that you can send your kid to cosmetology school. She'll graduate able to do her doll's hair herself, and yours too. Then you take the money you saved and go with your fancy new hair to buy a year's supply of añejo tequila and have some quality time with your friends while your kid goes outside and makes chalk art on the sidewalk, which is what she wanted to do in the first place before you set her in front of the television where she learned she was supposed to want a $100 doll.

They even have an American Girl Hospital. For $25, you can get a new arm. A new head: $38. At those prices it's cheaper to get a whole new doll than to Frankenstein one together out of parts. (Real humans are the same, by the way.) Of all the heads that need replacing, maybe the doll's is not atop the list.

The story right next to the one about dolls announced a new book: *Baby And Toddler Meals for Dummies*. It is the latest in the Dummy series, and tells you what to feed a baby. The book is $19.99, so it is definitely titled correctly. I was going to include a photo here of what God intended you to use to feed your baby and thus save you $19.99, but with my camera in hand I couldn't get any woman to lift up her sweater.

So maybe we need that dummy book after all, because a million girls have been taught by their mothers that if your baby is hungry, you fly her to Chicago for tea. ❦

I WANT IT SO BAD

W<small>HEN</small> I <small>WAS A KID</small>, I really, *really* wanted a Hot Wheels Super-Charger Racing set. I first laid eyes on it in the Sears catalog, which had a whole fat section devoted to toys I never saw in real life. I crafted a plan to trick my dad into buying it for me for Christmas: I pointed it out in the catalog, then sighed heavily that it was really too fancy for a regular kid like me, and that we didn't need to spend that kind of money anyway, and so I'd be perfectly satisfied with the cheaper, albeit not nearly as cool, Hot Wheels Dragster Set with Loop-The-Loop and Real Working Drag Chute.

Christmas came. I got the Dragster Set. I was stupefied.

So the following year when he asked what I wanted for Christmas, I chose a more direct approach. "Dad," I said firmly, "I really, *really* want an Atari." And that Christmas he bought an Atari — for my sister.

"Who *is* this man?" I wondered to myself.

Dad was always trying to teach me subtle life lessons, but I never did figure that one out. Maybe it boiled down to "If you want something bad enough, buy it yourself." Or maybe, "Get a haircut — I can't tell you from your sister."

I read in the newspaper that a local Senate candidate kicked in $1.4 million dollars of his own money to launch his primary campaign. I looked it up: a senator earns $162,000 a year, not counting bribes. Keeping in mind that this was still just the primary election, I would conclude that the candidate didn't have a good head for investing. But it turns out he was Vice Chairman of the Board of Ameritrade, an investment firm his dad founded, and they're doing just fine, thank you.

So I'm guessing he just really, *really* wants to be elected. If it were me, I'd go to my dad and say, "Please, *puhleeeeeeaahze* buy me that Senate seat. I promise I'll never, ever, ask for another office."

Of course, knowing my dad, I'd end up a Supreme Court Justice.

So maybe the hopeful candidate is going with the "If you want something bad enough, buy it for yourself" lesson. (I know the candidate does not need a haircut — he's already bald.)

It's not a bad plan. It's better than his challenger's, who was quoted as saying that illegal wiretapping "is the responsibility of the president, not the courts." That quote is even more startling when you learn that this man had been Nebraska's Attorney General. I presume, before the primary was over, someone hit him over the head with the Constitution.

The race was brutal. Our hero ended up spending a total of $12 million of his own money during the campaign. He lost in the primary, by 2-to-1.

As for my dad, a year later he gave me that Hot Wheels Super-Charger Racing Set after all. I had asked for a bike. ❦

THE ABOMINABLE SNOWSTORM

WHAT A GYP! All everybody talked about for three days was the Huge Snowstorm that was on its way. Nebraskans love to be threatened by weather. Never would a blizzard be more fun, because in spite of the promised *Twenty Inches!* and *Drifting Winds!* we knew the snow wouldn't linger long because it was already late in March, and we'd all be wearing shorts and thongs in a couple of weeks. (For people of my generation, thongs go on your feet. Flip-flops. Not that bastard child of underwear and dental floss, which nobody should wear, springtime or not.)

Blizzards bring out my nesting instincts. I scrounged up firewood, stocked food and wine, and made a fat vat of chili. Then I waited. I looked out the window. Storm should be here soon. By now, even. *A n y m i n u t e .* One by one the employees of my bar called: "Can we stay home?" Sure, why not — no one is going to go out for a beer in this weather anyway. We might as well just stay closed.

Any minute...

Just yesterday I had barely escaped my friend Yanna's farmhouse, where I had been working over the weekend helping her prepare a big sculpture to be cast in bronze. Snow and ice were screaming to the ground on a sharp, painful wind. Drifts on the road were so high my truck went airborne bouncing over them. I stopped for gas and went to the bathroom one last time just to make sure my bladder was empty. (You can't control your emotions, but you can limit the damage.) I plowed onward, powered by my male-endowed Stoic Idiocy.

Halfway home the snow thinned, the sky brightened, the roads cleared. I got home early.

I felt cheated. It was an omen.

Any minute...

I watched Chief Meteorologist Jim Flowers on the news. The Huge Snowstorm was to hit at three o'clock, but now it was past six. His smile was taut, pulling nearly to a grimace as he listed all the computer models they had run which unanimously said *Huge storm!* and he all but apologized that everybody was getting whumped but Omaha. He was clearly disappointed that there was no carnage. It appeared to me he was trying not to cry.

I gave up at 11:30pm. Full of pre-storm staples, wine and chili and fudge ice cream, I had done nothing but sit in front of the fire, watch *Casablanca* and write booze-inspired song lyrics. What a crummy night.

I couldn't even go to my own bar. Closed due to No Good Reason. If Chief Meteorologist Jim Flowers blames El Niño, I'll shoot him.

Yanna's farm got two and a half feet of snow. She was stranded for days in the middle of nowhere with nothing but a woodburning stove, homemade chicken soup, two cats, a guitar and a bottle of zinfandel. Lucky duck.

P.S. to word geeks: here is what the *Oxford American Dictionary* offered when I looked up "abominable" to make sure I was using the word correctly. I presume the entry was not supposed to be funny:

"1. *Abominable:* (adjective) Loathsome, detestable, hateful, odious, obnoxious, despicable, contemptible, damnable, diabolical, disgusting, revolting, repellant, repulsive, offensive, repugnant, abhorrent, reprehensible, atrocious, horrifying, execrable, foul, vile, wretched, base, horrible, awful, dreadful, appalling, nauseating, horrid, nasty, disagreeable, unpleasant, distasteful, informal, terrible, shocking, godawful, beastly, cursed.

"Antonym: Good." 🐭

HAPPY NEW YEAR

THE NEW YEAR'S EVE PARTY at my bar had been a great success. Our planning worked out well, surprise blizzard notwithstanding. Because of the storm, I figured everyone, including the staff, would stay safe at home, avoiding the inevitable skidfest of Drunken Car Hockey. I was prepared to drink a toast by myself in an empty bar, and I already had picked out a nice tequila with a float of Cointreau.

But despite the storm, customers filled the bar. The music was festive, and a long line of people eagerly waited to have their future revealed by a palm-reader we hired for the evening. I had wrenched my back shoveling snow right before the party, so the endless smile on my face was mostly a frozen-on grimace.

It was late when we finally closed up for the night and for the year, and we were all exhausted. I limped home, feet sore, back aching. I peeled off my clothes and creaked into bed, releasing a long sigh. I had put fresh sheets on the bed earlier to heighten this luxurious moment.

Just as I slid off the cliff of sleep, our security company woke me with a phone call: the burglar alarm was going off at the bar. I struggled to pump consciousness back into my brain, but I fell back asleep. Another call got through to me at 9am. The motion detectors were sounding. Somebody was in there. I had to drag my cranky, wincing, aching-tired ass out of bed and directly into the blowing snow. Happy Fucking New Year.

I presumed that, in my exhaustion, I had left the bar unlocked. By now a band of very lucky opportunists had helped themselves to my liquor. But when I arrived, all the doors were locked tight. I checked the alarm panel. The motion detectors had indeed gone off, twice. But the door alarms had not.

Doors locked, motion detectors going off — that could only happen...if...*Shit!* Someone was inside the whole time!

I don't talk about the ghosts at my bar much, because the second I do I have to sit for two hours while everyone else tells better ghost stories than mine. My ghosts are definitely second-string. I'm not sure they're even still there. But ghosts were a more pleasant explanation than meeting a Real Live Still Inside Burglar, so I clung to the ghost possibility.

It's a miserable task, poking and peeking around every dark, musty corner of a one-hundred-year-old bar basement, hoping to flush a hiding intruder. It sure does wake you right up.

Nothing was missing. Nothing disturbed. No tracks. No clues. Nobody was there.

So what set off the motion detectors? As I stood alone in the middle of the empty bar scratching my chin analytically, our legendary overpowered furnace kicked on. Its blustery wind resurrected from the dead all the New Year's Eve balloons, which began circling slowly around the room in an eerie, silent square dance.

I felt as if I was inside a snow globe. The motion detector went off.

A good belly laugh is a fine way to start a new year, and a pretty good way to exhale fear.

I stopped by the bar later that afternoon. The cleaning crew had swept up the confetti, straightened the chairs, shined everything back up. There was nary a trace of the New Year's Eve party, except for a few charming homemade decorations that I couldn't bear to take down yet. Before I left, I paused to pour a snifter of that tequila. I took a good look around, and raised a silent toast to the empty bar.　❧

PILLOW FLIGHT

I FELL DOWN THE STAIRS. It wasn't my first trip. I have long feet, and they occasionally ski off the step when I'm going down. Plus I'm tall, so my brain is far away from my feet. It takes longer for important Mayday messages to get back and forth. For this reason the brontosaurus had a brain in his head and another in his tail. He was too long for one brain. It worked, too. Archaeologists have never found brontosaurus bones at the bottom of the stairs.

I only have one brain. Occasionally I overshoot a step. My foot slips off and I go down on my back, my skeleton making that *brrrrink!* marimba sound as I slide down the wooden stairs.

This time was different. Laurie and Laura decided to host a Mediterranean dinner party, and they imagined it would be fun to move all the furniture out of the living room and have everyone sit on pillows. I don't know if people really eat like that in Mediterranea, but I know these two will never have a regular dinner party, with grilled bratwurst, potato chips and ketchup on paper plates, because that would cheat us out of the fun of moving a couch through a skinny doorway.

I offered to bring over my huge pile of big, bright pillows from my attic, left over from a once brilliant decorating scheme. Even with my long arms, I found it hard to gather up a stack of such squishy pillows, harder yet to keep ahold of them, harder still to see that first stair.

As I toppled head-first over the edge, my screams were muffled. The pillows were all over me. I felt like a sock in a clothes dryer. It was like being abused by the Sta-Puf Marshmallow Man: no real pain, but generally unpleasant.

When I was in high school I worked for a motel, washing bed sheets in an array of giant laundry machines. My friend Odee, the son of the motel owner, stopped by to visit me. Watching me work, he decided he could fit himself into one of the industrial-sized dryers. I dutifully helped him crawl in, tossed in a few pillowcases to complete the load, turned off the burner so he wouldn't wrinkle, and set him for ten minutes. Although I couldn't hear him through the glass door, it looked like he was having fun because he had the same expression on his face that people do when they ride the rollercoaster.

I was out getting a strawberry pop from the pop machine when the timer buzzed, so I was a little late in letting him out. His parents didn't allow him to swear, and he couldn't come up with any other words to say. I broke the awkward silence by noting that he looked fluffy.

I thought of Odee as I tumbled down the stairs. I had yet to manage a noise as I poofed to a landing. My daughter passed by on her way to the kitchen. She stepped gingerly over me, tippy-toe-ing through the scattered pillows, not asking for clarification. I suppose such sights don't surprise her anymore.

"I'm fine," I offered.

She replied, "Are we out of milk?" ❦